CELEBRATING THE SEASON OF ADVENT

Edited by ELTIN GRIFFIN OCarm

Celebrating
the season of
Advent

the columba press

the columba press

8 Lower Kilmacud Road, Blackrock, Co Dublin, Ireland

First edition 1986
Designed by Bill Bolger
Origination by Typeform Ltd., Dublin
Printed in Ireland by
Mount Salus Press, Dublin

ISBN: 0 948183 33 0

Contents

Preface

There is an atmosphere about the season of Advent that is unparallelled by any of the other seasons of the Church Year. As the late Clifford Howell SJ put it many years ago "It is an extraordinary blend of cheerfulness and sadness, of hope and fear, of longing with joy in possession." (*The Way*, October 1962). Among the Christian Churches, East and West, none can compare with the Roman Catholic tradition for sheer richness of expression during Advent. As any season journeys through history, it gathers a whole diversity of meanings to itself, a whole range of insight and feeling, poetic and mystical. The end result is a most beautiful and captivating synthesis. Pope John Paul II on his first visit to France at a special Mass in Lisieux quoted from a Polish philosopher, not too well known in this part of the world, Cyril Norwid: "the beautiful exists in order that it may enchant us for work."

The beautiful exists in the Advent liturgy. It may fail to enchant for work because most people tend to be overworked at this time of the year. The commercial world has got into its stride long before Advent. As the days go on, the buying and selling assume frenetic proportions. As Christmas approaches the demands on time and energy seem to increase with carol services in parishes, with nativity plays and other dramatic productions in schools, with office parties and staff social gatherings, with deadlines being announced for mailing overseas and for Santa himself, with the need to plan the Christmas fare and fun well in advance. Such hectic activity can lessen the ability to attend to what is coming across in the liturgy. That which should nourish our minds,

1

enrich our imaginations, free our hearts and give us fresh hope and new vision goes by unheeded. One begins to envy the monastic situation where we presume that unhurried pace allows one to savour and penetrate the depths of what is being celebrated, as the season mounts to a crescendo with the proclamation of the genealogy of Christ on December 17th and with the strains of the great O Antiphons expressing both longing and fulfillment as Christmas draws near.

We hope that this volume will act as a source of enlightenment for those who wish to explore the season of Advent more deeply, for preachers of the Word and for the growing numbers of laity who contribute towards the upbuilding of their local communities in their preparation of the liturgy. This volume was born of eight years' experience at the Gort Muire Conference Centre in Ballinteer, Co Dublin where the Carmelite Community hosted a number of Advent weekends. We had a full house every time and a great variety among those who addressed themselves to so many aspects of the season of Advent in their presentations. It has also been heartening to see the Advent season gradually come alive in parishes through greater emphasis on appropriate music and on the visual. My sincere thanks to all who have contributed to this volume. Inevitably, in a volume like this one, there is a certain repetition, a criss-crossing of ideas. The main issue is that all the contributors seem to be largely in agreement with each other — except on details of the Advent wreath!

Eltin Griffin, O Carm
Terenure College, Dublin 6.

The Spirit of Advent

Thomas McCarthy OP

The cycle of the different liturgical seasons in the Church's year could, perhaps not unfairly, be seen as a stylised resumé of some central Christian themes and concerns. Of course this cycle is closely bound up, too, with the historical events of the birth and death of Jesus of Nazareth. But has it not been remarked that it is futile that he was born so long ago in Bethlehem unless he is born again, today, in my heart? Whatever happened, what was done and written about was done 'for us and for our salvation'. That us, and this our, include the readers and writers of these Advent pages.

The human person and the human community is ever expectant, waiting. Sometimes looking forward with high expectation, sometimes awaiting the worst, awaiting in fear the day the disaster will come too close for comfort. As a rule, the optimistic, confident expectation retains a hue of realism; generally, too, that fear is not altogether terrifying. (If it were, it would succumb to paralysis or suicide.) At any rate, besides the expectations, life is also about living the present moment, for the present moment is the only moment at my disposal. And that present moment can become the moment of awakening. 'Now, I say, is the favourable time. This is the day of salvation.' Now what is it that awakens the present moment and makes it to be the day of salvation? The Advent of God. The approach of the Lord's footsteps. The nearness of his voice; the warmth of his hand.

Sometimes, of course, the language he speaks seems a distant and worthless babble; often, our heart-break and *angst* seem to be of no concern to him, and the language of the

Church seems to need interpretation before it can be of use.

This book will say, again and again, The Lord Comes. The Lord has come. And he comes at all times and in all circumstances. The Scriptures of the Hebrews and of the disciples of Jesus are full of testimonies of the believers' hope in his coming. The created world reflects the glory of God. In nature and its cycles, he comes. Man and woman were made in the image of God. Then there are the advents of the Lord in the lives and witness of his servants, Abraham, Jacob, Elijah, whose lives are understood as signs of the love and presence of the Lord. At times, too, there were what seemed like signs of the Lord being absent, of having abandoned his people. The people of Israel wondered where the Lord was, felt emptiness and loss, believed the Lord to have forsaken them. And their prophets confirmed that the Lord was, indeed, absent: he was at a distance, but it was a gap of the people's doing, not God's invention. *They* had turned their backs on the Lord who loved them. Through Adam's fall, and the people's subsequent sins, by means of the weakening of love and obedience, they were unable to stand the presence of God's love, and turned aside to other gods, other paths. And he, with careful love, called Israel back, and loved her as in the days of their first love.

Advent is often seen as a time of preparation, of repentance in advance of the Lord's coming. This is right and fitting. It is also good news. We must seek the Lord, who is all the time awaiting us. Advent must also be marked by a spirit that searches again for the footprints of Jesus in human lives and in world history. There must be within us an advent frame of mind, with ears open for the voice of that divine lover, whose advances are compelling, and also demanding. In Advent, the Christian community sees the beloved arrive at the window. There is, besides, also the menacing spectre of the Fourth Gospel over us: he came to his own, and his own received him not. Well, again he comes. And again. He is all around us to be seen, to be welcomed, to be fed and clothed, to be cared for and protected. It has been said that

4

hundreds of people crowd into the pews on a Sunday morning and are again appalled at the suffering of Christ all those years ago, in a foreign country and remain unmoved by the manifold suffering of their own twentieth-century neighbours . . . the squalid poverty of so many in our cities; the discrimination against the weak and against minorities; the loveless society so often faced by those who need community and love. What good news have we for the poor in our society who cry out in their misery or boredom? If the coming of Christ brings a message for the bereaved, the jobless, the discarded and retarded, is the Christian church announcing that message to them? Is the company of his disciples incarnate, as the Lord was? Can the world say of us as it could accurately have said of the Lord, 'This, at last, is bone of my bones and flesh of my flesh'?

The spirit of Advent is one of generosity, of giving in return for, in thanksgiving for, the gift we have joyfully received, and that is the Lord God of hosts in physical shape. God is as close to the world as a hand-shake is. Truly Emmanuel. The Lord has wished to offer humanity a sign of peace. It is a boy . . . Thanks be to God.

Origins and Development of Advent

Vincent Ryan OSB

When the feast of the nativity of the Lord was introduced to Rome in the early years of the fourth century, it was celebrated as a simple memorial and was not preceded by a period of preparation. It was not until about the middle of the sixth century, by which time Christmas had become a major solemnity almost on a par with Easter, that the Roman Advent made its appearance.[1]

It is outside of Rome, especially in Spain and Gaul, that the earliest form of Advent appears. The Council of Saragossa in Spain in 380 refers to a three-week period of preparation extending from 17 December to the feast of the Epiphany. It urges the faithful to be assiduous in going to church daily during this time. The Epiphany, like Easter, was a time for the conferring of baptism, and this suggests that the weeks of preparation were conceived mainly in function of the sacrament of initiation. But for all the faithful this was a time of prayer, ascetic effort and assembly in church.[2]

Towards the end of the fifth century in Gaul, the three-week period of preparation was extended to forty days. Our earliest witness is Bishop Perpetuus of Tours (†490) whose regulations on fasting during this period have been preserved. Beginning on the feast of St Martin, 11 November, the period was known as the *Lent of St Martin*. The name was well chosen for this season since it was strongly penitential in character and lasted forty days. By this time Christmas had replaced Epiphany as the terminus of the time of preparation.[3]

Advent in Rome

The Roman church did not see the need for a prolonged pre-Christmas fast such as existed in Spain and Gaul. When the season of Advent eventually made its appearance, it was liturgical rather than ascetical in character. From the start it was directly oriented to Christmas, not Epiphany, and took its whole meaning from that feast. It had no connection with baptism.

Advent was indeed a late development in Rome. It is surprising to learn that Pope St Leo the Great (440-61), who in his preaching developed such a rich theology of Christmas, does not seem to have known a time of Advent. Our earliest witnesses to a Roman Advent are the liturgical books, especially the sacramentaries. Of the latter, the Veronese or Leonine Sacramentary (6th century), which is the earliest of these compilations, does not yet have this liturgical season. The Galasian and Gregorian Sacramentaries, however, which represent a more developed liturgy, provide formularies for the Sundays of Advent.[4]

The primitive form of the Roman Advent, represented by the Galasian sacramentary, had six weeks before Christmas. This was the practice of some other churches, and is still a feature of the Milanese rite. It was during the pontificate of Pope St Gregory the Great that the number of weeks was reduced to four, and that has remained the tradition ever since. No doubt this great pontiff had sound pastoral reasons for curtailing the season by two weeks. Liturgically, he may have judged it inappropriate that Advent should have the same duration as Lent. Whatever his motives were, we may have our own reasons today for preferring the earlier tradition. In the pressurised society in which we live, three or four weeks seem all too short a time to assimilate the riches of the Advent liturgy.

The meaning of Advent

In its earliest form Advent was basically a preparation for Christmas. It focussed on the liturgical commemoration of

Christ's birth. Within a fairly short time, however, it acquired an eschatological character. From the beginning of the seventh century Advent was understood not only as a time of preparation for the Christmas solemnity but also, and especially, as a time of waiting and expectancy for the return of Christ in glory.[5] In other western churches this eschatological thrust became even more pronounced. It was a characteristic feature of the Gallican liturgy, and this may have come about or been developed through the influence of Irish missionary monks who, in their preaching, laid such great stress on the coming of the Lord in judgement and on the need to do penance. In the Advent prayers of the Old Spanish or Mozarabic liturgy the eschatological note is preponderant.

The word *Advent (Adventus)* designated originally not the period of preparation, but the feast of Christmas itself. The coming of Christ in the flesh and the liturgical commemoration of that event was the *adventus Domini*, the advent of the Lord. And since in the New Testament the word *adventus* translated the Greek *parousia,* it was natural that in its Christian usage the term should include in its connotation the second coming of Christ at the end of time. Gradually the word *adventus* assumed a new, distinctly liturgical meaning: it came to be applied to the weeks of preparation for Christmas. From being a time *ante adventum* (before the coming) this season became a time *in adventu*, a season of preparation for Christmas and of expectation of the glorious return of Christ.[6]

Many of us today find it difficult to grapple with the idea of two comings, juxtaposed or superimposed in the Advent liturgy. For the fathers of the Church, with their unified vision of the mysteries of Christ, this posed no problem. Pope St Leo the Great, for example, in his sermons for Christmas and Epiphany, leads his hearers and readers beyond the mystery of the incarnation and manifestation to the contemplation of Christ now enthroned in glory and to his return at the end of the ages.[7] We need to recover this comprehensive view of things. As an older commentator has well written: "The mystery of Christ's coming is something indivisible. His appearance on earth and the *parousia* are two aspects of a single redemptive coming which is not yet completed: he who came will come again, and he has told us to watch and wait."[8] The Church evokes the coming of Christ in all its aspects, past, present and future. This season recalls the coming on earth of the incarnate Word, deepens our awareness of Christ's presence in the Church today and heightens our hope and longing for his return. It is a kind of "anticipation of the feast of Christmas, viewing the mystery of the incarnation in the light of its full and final achievement".[9]

Fusion of Roman and Gallican liturgies

As to its essential form and structure the development of the Roman Advent was completed by the eighth century. But it was to be profoundly influenced by the very different spirit of the Gallican Advent which, as already noted, was markedly penitential in character. The liturgy of the Roman Advent retained its message of joyful hope, but some of the ceremonial expressions of joy were suppressed, and the regulations concerning the observance of this season were decidedly Lenten in character. Not that the Roman Advent did not also include a note of penance, but in the positive sense of a call to conversion and renewal of life. That note is sounded in the readings of the Sunday eucharist which summon us to "prepare a way for the Lord", and to "cast off the works of darkness". The Gallican Advent stressed the more negative and restrictive aspects of penance.

This contact of the Roman with the Gallican and Frankish liturgies had its positive side. It was a question of "loss and gain". Certainly there resulted an enrichment in the repertory of chant, hymnody and ritual, even if the latter became over elaborate and dramatic. Among the most splendid additions to the Roman Advent must be included the O Antiphons or Greater Antiphons. They have been in use in our western

9

liturgy since the time of Charlemagne. Amalarius of Metz (780-850) attributed their composition to an anonymous cantor who probably lived in the eighth century.[10]

It is interesting to learn that it was only in the eighth or ninth centuries that the tradition was established of commencing the liturgical year with the first Sunday of Advent. We shall return later to this point. But it is now time to turn our attention to liturgical traditions other than those of the western Church. How do Christians of eastern Christianity celebrate Advent?

The eastern tradition

In none of the eastern Churches does Advent exist as a distinct liturgical season. The latter is a characteristically western creation and one of which we can be justifiably proud. Nevertheless, in its own manner eastern Christianity, both ascetically and liturgically, prepares for the celebration of the birth of the Lord and his manifestation. Here we consider only one of these liturgies, that of the Byzantine tradition, which is the best known and most widely practised. Since the churches practising this rite follow the teaching of the first seven Ecumenical Councils, they belong to what is known as the Orthodox Church.[11]

Fasting is taken very seriously by Orthodox Christians. They begin their ascetical preparation for Christmas on November 15 with what is known as the Christmas fast or the fast of St Philip. Like the lenten fast it lasts forty days but is not quite as strict. This is a long established practice in the Greek Orthodox Church, certainly going back to the ninth century. The fast on Christmas Eve is very strict. It should not be inferred from this that the spirit of the Orthodox Advent is merely penitential. It is one of the charisms of Orthodox spirituality to be able to combine fasting with spontaneous joy. This is true of the Lenten and Christmas fasts. The following short text from Matins of December 21 well expresses the joyful mood in which the Byzantine churches prepare for the birth of Christ:

The Creator, the Wisdom of God, draws near,
the mist of the prophets' promise is dispersed.
Joy clears the skies
Truth is resplendent
The dark shadows are dispelled
The gates of Eden are opened
Adam dances in exultation:
Our Creator and God wills to fashion us anew.[12]

The liturgical preparation for Christmas begins on the second Sunday preceding the feast. This is known as the Sunday of the Ancestors of the Lord. This commemorates the patriarchs and prophets of the Old Covenant from Adam to John the Baptist. In common with the Roman Advent the Byzantine pre-Christmas liturgy is prophetic; but the list of those who foretold or prepared the way for the Messiah is more extensive than our own, since it includes Moses, Aaron, Joshua, Samuel, David, and many others. It makes mention of "all the ancestors according to the flesh, those before the law and those under the law".

The Sunday which immediately precedes Christmas is known as the Sunday of the Fathers or of the Genealogy. On this day the Church seeks to bring into the joy of the nativity all the just men and women who lived before Christ. Again the list is extensive, running from Adam to St Joseph. It includes some of the great women of the Old Testament: Sarah, Rebecca, Hannah, Miriam, Ruth and others. They belong to that great "cloud of witnesses" whose faith and constancy we must imitate. The gospel reading for this Sunday is the genealogy of Jesus Christ according to St Matthew. Its purpose is to affirm that Jesus, the Son of God, has come in the flesh as a real human being and truly one of our race.

From December 20 begins the immediate preparation for the festival. These five days are known as the forefeast. They are not only a preparation for, but already a foretaste of, the mystery of Christmas day. The liturgy focuses strongly and clearly on the reality of the incarnation and birth of the Lord as defined and taught by the great councils of the Church, in particular that of Chalcedon.

The services for Christmas Eve are even longer than those of the feast itself. The Church sets before the faithful the whole panorama of the nativity and plumbs the depths of its mystery. This allows for a more relaxed and prayerful assimilation of the fruits of the feast on Christmas day itself. As a monk of the eastern Church observes: "December 24th speaks to us of the same things as December 25th, but the 24th is a preparation, an instruction, a praise which welcomes the event; the 25th is the fulness, the fruition, the praise which crowns the accomplished fact".[13]

Unlike the western Advent, so markedly eschatological in character, the idea of Christ's second coming is not a pronounced feature of the orthodox liturgy of preparation. At most one could say that the notion is implicit in the songs, hymns and readings of this time. Expectation of the parousia comes to the fore at other times of the year, notably during the first three days of Holy Week.[14]

Orthodox christians are just as aware as we of the western tradition of the intimate connection between the first and final coming of Christ. A visual expression of this is provided by the artistic setting of the liturgy. Before the altar on either side of the "royal gates", are set corresponding icons, one depicting Mary and her child, the other representing the Lord Jesus in glory. In the minds of the faithful participating in the liturgy, these two comings are held together at all times and cannot be separated.[15]

Popular piety during Advent

Returning to the western Church we now consider some expressions of popular devotion during the season of Advent. My source of information here is a study of the folklore of Advent and Christmas by the American Jesuit, Fr X Weiser.[16] As a general observation it is worth stating from the start that these pious customs are in harmony with the liturgy and reinforce its message. Also it is noteworthy that they exhibit a spirit that is joyful rather than ascetic and penitential.

No doubt the best loved symbol of Advent, and the one we are most familiar with, is the Advent wreath. Around this symbol, in church and home, there has evolved an expressive prayer ritual or liturgy of the home. Its origins go back to pre-christian times, to the sun-worshipping tribes of northern Europe. It was one of the many symbols of light which were used at the end of November and early December, that time of year when our pagan ancestors celebrated the month of Yule by lighting torches and fires. To appease the sun-god and to ensure his return in the darkest time of the year, they took what may have been a cart wheel, wound with greens and decorated with lights, and offered it to the deity.

This pagan custom survived into christian times. Medieval people kept many of these fire and light symbols as popular traditions with pagan or superstitious overtones. It was in the sixteenth century in eastern Germany that the custom was Christianised, so to speak, and the Advent wreath made its appearance in people's homes as a religious symbol of Advent. The custom spread rapidly throughout the whole of Germany, and became popular with Catholics and Lutherans alike. It spread to other countries in Europe. Its adoption in English speaking countries is witnessed to only in recent times, but now it is firmly established and very popular in Britain, Ireland and North America.

In the ritual of lighting an extra candle each week on the Advent wreath, we give expression to the hope and longing of the people of the Old Covenant for a redeemer, and the gradual realisation of God's promises through the prophets and finally John the Baptist and the Virgin Mary. The wreath itself, symbol of victory and glory, symbolises the fulness of time, the birth of Christ and the glory of his coming.[17]

A custom we may not be familiar with in these islands is the Christmas Novena. In countries of South America the nine days preceding Christmas are devoted to a popular novena in honour of the Holy Child *(La Novena del Nina)*.

There is first the setting up of the crib in the decorated church. All the figures are there except the Child Jesus who will be brought in on Christmas Day. Each day there takes place an office of the novena consisting of popular prayers and chants in which great numbers of people, including the children, take part.

Pre-Christmas novenas are not unknown in Europe. In some central European countries there has existed into our own times the beautiful devotion of the Golden Nights. It was given this name because it took place during the hours of darkness, either after nightfall or before dawn. In Alpine regions it was the custom to have a picture or statue of the Blessed Virgin carried from house to house on each successive day of the novena. At the close of the day the family and neighbours gathered round this representation of Mary and said prayers and sang hymns in her honour. Then the young people would carry it in procession to the next homestead where it was received with due honour and again venerated by its new hosts. And so it continued each day until Christmas. It was also the custom in many parts of Europe for rural Catholics to attend a pre-dawn Mass on the mornings of the Golden Nights. The liturgy was that of the votive Mass of the Blessed Virgin during Advent.

In these devotions there is evidently a strong awareness of the presence of Mary in the Advent season. This accords with the Church's liturgy especially in the time of immediate preparation for Christmas. Irish people expressed their devotion to Mary by a more frequent recitation of the rosary (*Coróin Mhuire*, Mary's crown) during Advent. The more devout among them would recite, in addition to the family rosary, extra rosaries of their own. The ideal — and I am unaware of the special significance of this — was to attain a total of four thousand Hail Marys before Christmas!

Fr Weiser's appreciation of these various folk-customs does not extend to present-day practices which, by anticipating the festive season, deprive the feast itself of its true significance and joyful radiance. Advent has become an ex-

tended shopping spree and we soon become weary of a
surfeit of Christmas carols, some of them sentimental and
secular. Let there be joyful anticipation certainly, but let
us not pre-empt the Christmas celebration by untimely
festivity. Even the best of our carols should not be sung too
early in the season. After all, observes our author, we do not
sing our Easter alleluias on Ash Wednesday or Good Friday!

Advent since Vatican II

The renewal of the liturgy effected by the second Vatican
Council, did not fundamentally alter the season of Advent.
Its structure remained unaltered, its traditional features
were respected. Liturgical directives emanating from Rome
sought to clarify further the nature and purpose of this season and to determine more precisely its spirit. In what
pertains to the four weeks of Advent, the liturgical renewal
has brought about a tremendous enrichment of the texts of
the lectionary, missal and breviary,

As for the spirit of Advent, we are now left in no doubt
that this is a season of joyful hope, not a time of penance.
Previously there was some ambiguity about this, and there
was a tendency to impose a penitential discipline on this
season, thus assimilating it to Lent. Now the General Norms
for the Liturgical Year and Calendar declare Advent to be
a "season of joyful and spiritual expectation" (no. 39), and
in the accompanying commentary it is stated explicitly that
this "is no longer to be considered a penitential season."
Some vestiges of the older observance do remain, such as
the suppression of the Gloria at Sunday Mass and the wearing
of purple vestments. Both these practices were transmitted
from Gaul to Rome in the twelfth century. The commentary
explains that the Gloria is dropped "in order to allow it to
ring out with certain freshness at Christmas", and, likewise,
the sobriety of colour will make the white vestments appear
all the more brilliant on Christmas day.

The season of Advent has been given a more clear-cut
structure. Its essential unity has been maintained, while its

twofold character has been made more clearly discernible. Clarifying articles 39 to 42 of the Calendar, which treat of Advent, the commentary adds: "The liturgical texts of Advent display a unity demonstrated by the almost daily reading of the prophet Isaiah. Nevertheless, two parts of Advent can be clearly distinguished, each with its own significance, as the new prefaces clearly illustrate. From the first Sunday of Advent until December 16 the liturgy expresses the eschatological character of Advent and urges us to look for the second coming of Christ. From December 17-24, the daily propers of the Mass and Office prepare more directly for the celebration of Christmas."

From a consideration of the form of the Advent liturgy, we move to a brief examination of its content. We take in turn the lectionary, the missal and the breviary. As for the first, it constitutes a veritable mine of biblical spirituality. Its richness can be the better appreciated by comparing it with what went before. In the lectionary of the missal of Pius V, there were only nineteen readings provided for Advent. In the lectionary promulgated by Pope Paul VI in 1969, there are no fewer than seventy five pericopes for the pre-Christmas season. If one takes into account the three-year cycle of readings, it means that we now have twelve liturgical celebrations for the four Sundays of Advent. These celebrations have an organic unity and are complementary to one another. From Sunday to Sunday there is a progression of thought and theme: the first two Sundays announce the coming of the Lord in judgement, the third expresses the joy of a coming already very near, the fourth and last "appears as a Sunday of the fathers of the Old Testament and the Blessed Virgin Mary, in anticipation of the birth of Christ".[18] As for the weekday readings, they are adapted to the theology expressed in the Sunday celebration which preceded them.[19]

Fr Gaston Fontaine, one of the compilers of our present lectionary, has given an account of the immense research which lay behind the selection of readings for Advent.[20]

An exhaustive study of all the lectionaries of the western Church covering a period of 1500 years was undertaken, and from this collection a choice of all that was best and most traditional was made. Some of these readings are traditionally Roman and would have been familiar to the faithful of Rome in the time of Pope St Gregory the Great, and even before his time. Others are drawn from the traditions of the Old Spanish, Gallican and other western Churches. The result is a treasury of incomparable riches which enables the Church of our day to celebrate the *adventus domini* in all its phases, past, present and future.

The missal too, in its euchology for Advent, has been greatly enriched. Where formerly there were proper prayers only for the Sundays and December Ember Days, now we have a proper collect for each day of Advent. In addition there is a wider selection of *super oblata* and post-communion prayers, two fine prefaces where none existed before, and a solemn blessing for this season. The twenty nine collects also appear in the breviary as the prayers of the day. What is of special interest in this series is that it includes a number of splendid prayers from a source hitherto unknown to the Roman liturgy, the so-called Rotulus of Ravenna. These prayers date from the sixth century or even earlier, and combine theological depth with an elevated literary style. While the Roman collects (mainly from the Galasian Sacramentary) are directed to the second coming of Christ, these are focussed more directly on the coming of Christ in the flesh and express the humble attitude of faith before the mystery of the incarnation.[21]

The liturgy of the hours has likewise been renewed. Happily, nothing of real value in the old breviary has been discarded. The familiar antiphons and responsories, which give such a joyful and lyrical note to this season, have been retained. They now nurture the prayer life of the growing numbers who pray *The Divine Office or Daily Prayer*. The great O Antiphons, popularised through their use in paraliturgies and acclamations in the Mass, herald the approach of Christmas for the people of God as a whole.

It is in the office of readings that the greatest gains have been made. The scripture pericopes provide a daily semi-continuous reading from Isaiah. The patristic and other ecclesiastical readings complement this. They constitute an anthology of spiritual texts ranging in time from St Iranaeus to St John of the Cross and St Charles Borromeo. And since Advent is a time of hope and joy, the inclusion of extracts from the constitution *Gaudium et Spes,* which articulates the aspirations of all men and women, is a welcome addition.

These various authors urge us to prepare for the coming of Christ by the exercise of faith, hope and an ardent desire for, and love of, God. They ponder the mystery of the two comings, and, with Bernard and Borromeo, speak of a third, intermediate coming, which is the spiritual advent of Christ to each individual soul. Their vision extends beyond Advent to the mystery of Christmas itself. The great themes of the Christmas-Epiphany liturgy are already intimated in the patristic readings of Advent: the saving incarnation, the renewal of the image of God in man, the "wonderful exchange", the mystery of divine love which must be reciprocated. These thoughts we will savour and ponder at greater depth during the Christmas season. Summing up the message of these breviary readings, the late Fr Henry Ashworth writes: "During Advent the Christian prepares himself to receive the grace of salvation which will be given to him in celebrating the historical event of the mystery. But the incarnation is the beginning of a process which is not yet finished. Christ will return in glory to crown his work of salvation".[22]

In conclusion to this essay, I raise what may appear to be a technical point. Does the first Sunday of Advent really mark the beginning of the liturgical year? As we have seen, this has been the tradition in the Roman Church from about the ninth century and perhaps a little before that. A passage in the Liturgy Consitution of Vatican II seemed to imply that Advent was to be viewed as the conclusion rather than the beginning of the Church year. Article 102 reads: "Within the cycle of the year she (the Church) unfolds the whole mystery of Christ from the incarnation and nativity to the ascension, Pentecost and the expectation of the blessed hope of the coming of the Lord." In spite of this statement, the Roman Calendar and the revised liturgical books have maintained the centuries old tradition. One has to begin somewhere, and the first Sunday of Advent provides a convenient beginning to the Church year. From a liturgical point of view, however, one could argue that the ecclesiastical year begins with the Easter season rather than with the Christmas cycle. Whatever view one favours, it is important to remember that the Church year is eschatological rather than chronological, that we are dealing with liturgical time and not enacting a mystery play. Advent prepares us for the final coming of the Lord. Its symbol, as Fr Pierre Jounel suggests, is the empty throne depicted in the mosaics of Rome and Ravenna, waiting for the return of Christ to take possession of his kingdom.

NOTES

1. For the history of the Roman Advent I have followed J Hild, "L'Avent" in *La Maison-Dieu* 59 (1959), pp.10-24. Also consulted: P Jounel, "L'Avent" in *L'Eglise en Priere* edited by A G Martimort, Tournai, 1965, pp.753-57; W O'Shea, "Advent" in *New Catholic Encylopedia,* and A Adam, *The Liturgical Year* (New York, 1981), pp 130-38.
2. Hild, work cited, pp.13-14.
3. Hild, work cited, p 15.
4. For a description of the sacramentaries, see Martimort, *L'Eglise en Priere,* pp 287-96.

5. Hild, work cited, pp 18-19. In the official commentary to the Revised Liturgical Calendar it is stated: "It (Advent) was instituted to prepare the people for the celebration of Christmas, and shortly afterwards acquired an eschatological character."

6. Hild, pp 17-19. See also "Day of the Lord" in *Dictionary of Biblical Theology*.

7. See J Gaillard, "Noel, *memoria* ou mystère" in *La Maison-Dieu* 59 (1959), pp 37-59. I treat of this in *Advent to Epiphany* (Dublin, 1983), pp 10-12.

8. F Nogues, "Avent et avenement d'apres les anciens Sacramentaires" in *Questions Liturgiques et Paroissiales* 5 (1937), p 240.

9. W O'Shea in his study "Advent" in *New Catholic Encylopedia*.

10. Cited by M Huglo, "O Antiphons" in *New Catholic Encyclopedia*.

11. For this section I have relied mainly on J Dalmais, "Le Temps de preparation a Noel dans les liturgies Syrienne et Byzantine" in *LMD* 59 (1959), pp 25-36. Also consulted: *The Year of Grace of the Lord* by a Monk of the Eastern Church (London, 1980), pp 45-65; T Hopko, *The Winter Pascha* (New York, 1984), pp 9-93. Texts of the Forefeast in *The Festal Menaion* (London, 1969), translated by Mother Mary and K Ware, pp 199-251.

12. Quoted by T Hopko, *The Winter Pascha,* p 83.

13. *The Year of Grace of the Lord,* pp 59-60.

14. Hopko, work cited, p 90.

15. Hopko, work cited, p 91.

16. "Le Folklore de l'Avent et de Noel" in *La Maison-Dieu* 59 (1959), pp 104-31.

17. I treat of this in *Advent to Epiphany,* pp 19-21.

18. From the Commentary on the Roman Calendar, section 2, "The Advent Season".

19. For biblico-liturgical reflections on these readings, and also useful historical background, see A Nocent, *The*

Liturgical Year (Minnesota, Liturgical Press, 1977), Vol. 1, pp 95-161 and 167-77.

20. "L'Avent dans les Lectionnaires Latin" in *Notitiae* 173 (1980), pp 605-15. See also his earlier studies, "Le lectionnaire au temps de l'Advent", *Notitiae* 66 (1971), pp 304-17, and 67 (1971), pp 364-76.

21. For a study of these Advent prayers and an account of the work involved in translating them for *The Divine Office,* see the article of my confrère Fr Placid Murray, "The Glenstal-Headingley Collects" in *Life and Worship* (July 1973), pp 10-15.

22. "Themes of the Patristic Liturgy for Advent, Christmas, Epiphany" in *Hallel* (Advent 1975), pp 235-66. This is a translation of the article which was published originally in Italian in *Rivista-Liturgica* 5 (1972), pp 677-705.

Art in Advent

Stephanie Brophy

If I were asked what is the overall theme for our church activities during Advent, I would say:

Slow down, listen and live.

So often this great feast can sneak up on us while we are caught up in a mad whirl of shopping, presents, parties, cooking, gifts etc. and be gone without leaving any impression except that of weariness and utter fed-upness with Christmas music, fairies, Santa Claus, reindeer and jaded decorations.

In order to counteract this, and in an effort to offer the Church's more sensible and leisurely approach, we as a team in a centre city church planned a programme of such a nature as to catch the eyes of all who pass by or visit our church. Hopefully in the true Advent spirit these efforts would play on the mind, heart and senses of over anxious shoppers so that they, at least, may be encouraged to slow down, listen and live.

Keeping the season of Advent in the liturgical year is a privilege but one that demands much imagination and hard work. Early in September, it is advisable to set up a committee from as many sections of the community as possible. Through reflecting and sharing ideas on the readings of the four Sundays this group could discover the main themes of Advent and the best possible ways to bring the story of the Incarnation before the people and to develop this through visual aids.

Banners for each of the four Sundays could be decided.

The design and colours should be striking and well planned as a whole, building up each week in their contribution to the final decor of the church in its blaze of colour on Christmas night.

For example:

The first Sunday of Advent

Readings: Matthew   24:37-44
          Mark   13:33-37
          Luke   21:25-28, 34-36.

Theme: *Watch, Root of Jesse*   (Jer 33:14-16)
          Vigilant waiting for the Lord (Rom 13:11-14)

The second Sunday of Advent

Readings: Matthew   3:1-12
          Mark   1:1-8
          Luke   3:1-6

Theme: *Prepare, Fill the valleys*
          Warnings of John the Baptist

The third Sunday of Advent

Readings: Matthew   11:2-11
          John   1:6-8, 19-28
          Luke   3:10-18

Theme: *Christ, the Anointed one*
          Joy   (1 Thess 5:16-24)
          Patience   (James 5:7-10)

The fourth Sunday of advent

Readings: Matthew   1:18-24
          Luke   1:26-45

Theme: *Mary, Incarnation of the Word*
          Marana'tha

These are by no means the only themes that will arise. Tapping the mine of expertise in any group usually calls forth the rich ore of creativity, art, and perhaps an unexpected wealth and depth of thought.

We make our banners from felt, with contrasting lettering also in felt. Also available is a type of contact paper with a felt finish which is easy to manage and is very effective. The original outlay may be expensive but in the long run it is a better bargain. There is no waste in felt, for even the smallest pieces can be utilised. Copydex is a very good adhesive.

In our centre city church for Advent, we set out to emphasise the Incarnation of the Word — Christ our Saviour, God among us. As a divine person, he is the Light of the World, while as a human he has earthly ancestors as seen in the Bible.

Two contrasting symbols illustrating these themes of Christ, the Light of the World and Son of David are visibly expressed in the Advent wreath and the Advent tree (Jesse).

The Advent Wreath

It was in the western Church that the tradition of the Advent wreath grew. It celebrates the coming of the eternal Light into a world "sitting in darkness and the shadow of death" (Lk 1:78). This brightly wound wreath expresses our conviction that Christ will always come into the world as its true light.

Symbolism of the Wreath

The *circular shape* symbolises the coming of the Lord, in the past in flesh, in the present in grace, in the future in glory.

The *evergreens* are a sign of our hope for salvation. Green is the Church's colour for hope. We are reminded of the everlasting life and love that comes to us from God through Jesus Christ.

The *candles* (three purple and one rose-coloured) are the Light which "shines in the darkness," coming progressively as each week another candle is lit.

The *purple candles* (for the 1st, 2nd & 4th weeks) symbolise repentance and conversion, clearing away the mountains and filling in the valleys.

The *rose-coloured candle* (3rd week — formerly it was Gaudete Sunday) is a sign of our joy that the Lord is always near.

We usually make our Advent wreath in the week after the celebration of Christ the King. A few years ago, a large frame of wood and wire was professionally made with four candle holders fitted into the base. (This is stored from year to year). Since it is important that the Advent wreath can be seen from the end of the church, the frame we use is about 3' in diameter. The frame should be strong enough to support the 4 large candles; with a support for the final white candle which may be added for Christmas.

We found that the tilting of the large wreath towards the front was more effective than the horizontal view.

When decorating the Advent wreath, we wrap wide red ribbon round and round the wreath, and finish it off with a generous and artistically-arranged bow.

The ceremony of lighting the candles varies as to time and content, and has as many possibilities as the liturgy group of the parish decides. Prayer of the Sunday may be chosen or a similar prayer composed following the progressive theme of the four weeks.

The Jesse Tree
The Root of Jesse text from Isaiah 11:7, "A shoot shall sprout from the stump of Jesse and from his roots a bud shall blossom", inspired an American nun in 1949 to develop the family tree theme into the tree which became known as the Jesse Tree — Jesse was the father of David, the ancestor of Jesus.

We usually start at the end of November when a few stalwart members of our team set about felling and drawing home a huge 25' tree — for that is roughly the height of our church. The tree is placed in the sanctuary and makes its appearance during the first week of Advent — hopefully to catch the eye of the first Christmas shoppers 'from the country'. Anchored in a large barrel, which is camouflaged with cut-off branches it indeed looks very impressive. Lights, a reminder of Christ the Light of the World, are fitted at this stage but are not switched on until Christmas night.

The Jesse Tree is decorated with symbols of Jesus' ancestors and events or happenings in their lives, as recorded in the Bible — all of which found their fulfillment in Jesus Christ.

Symbols may be made most effectively from aeroboard or polystyrene. No great skill is needed as the simplest images are the most effective. Starting at the base of the tree we place symbols of creation and as the days and weeks go by other symbols are added, representing God's loving care of his chosen people and their deliverance from bondage. The last symbol, the Chi-Ro or PX sign is mounted on the topmost branch, on Christmas Eve.

Explanation of all that is happening is given verbally from the lectern at the daily Masses and, in greatest detail, they can be found on the display boards at the side of the church.

Ideas for these symbols are endless but we must be careful not to abuse our creativity. It is also important that the symbols are artistically and delicately made and presented.

In our heart of hearts we must acknowledge that Advent is a time for tradition. Tradition means that we remember what we have received and hand on that memory. It is not a lifeless repetition of what we heard — or thought we experienced — as children. Now we are part of it and we hand it on so that our children can be part of it in their turn. Here is a wonderful visual aid for true, teachable moments and what a joy it is to see the many visitors stroll through the church at a quiet time and pause in wonder at the magnificent sight of the huge tree, dotted all over with various symbols that call for explanation and scripture references. The children especially gaze in rapture and exclaim in the popular expression of the day, "Brilliant!"

The Jesse Tree is a celebration, an educational device derived from the figure of Jesse, the father of King David. It is a graphic representation of the genealogy of Jesus Christ, prepared in Advent to be enjoyed at Christmas.

Appropriate symbols from scripture readings during Advent are as follows:

Creation	Gen 1:1-2:2	world; sun; stars; animals; plants; birds etc
Fall & Promise	Gen 3:1-15	tree with fruit; serpent; angel with sword
Noah	Gen 6:9-22	ark; waves; olive branch; pairs of animals
	7:17-19	waves
	8:6-22	dove; olive branch
	9:8-17	rainbow
Abraham	Gen 12:1-5	shepherd's crook
	13:18	oak tree
Isaac	Gen 22:1-19	donkey; bundles of sticks; knife; altar with fire; ram; sand; stars
Jacob	Gen 28:10-18	ladder; angel; stone
Joseph	Gen 37:2-36	coloured coat; sheaf of wheat; pyramid
Moses	Ex 2:1-10	basket
	3:1-12	burning bush
	12:1-20	passover lamb; bread
	14:15-31	paths through waters
	16:1-16	manna; quails
	19	commandments on stone tablets
Joshua	Jos 6:1-21	trumpets
Ruth	Ruth 1:1-22	sheaf of wheat

David	1 Sam 16:1-13	horn of oil
	1 Sam 17:40-52	sling
	1 Sam 18:10	harp
	2 Sam 7:8-16	crown; 6-pointed star
Solomon	1 Kings 3:4-15	heart
	8:1-7	Ark
	10-29	temple
Judith	Jud 9,10,11	mirror, knife
Isaiah	Is 1:1-6	scroll
	16-20	red and white wool
Jeremiah	Jer 1:1-10	hand touching mouth
	31:31-34	love
Ezekiel	Ezek 11:17-21	angels' wings; wheels
	18:21-32	
Daniel	Dan 3:85-96	three men in fire
	6:11-28	a man; sealed book

Coming of Jesus

Trinity	Rom 5:1-5	triangle
Holy Spirit	1 Cor 12: 3-7, 12-13	dove
Gabriel	Lk 1:11,19, 26-29	angel; trumpet
Zechariah	Lk 1:5-25, 57-66	smoking incense; sealed lips
Elizabeth	Lk 1:39-45	old woman with baby
John the Baptist	Mt 11:7-15	desert; locusts; honey
Joseph	Mt 1:18-25	carpenter's tools

Mary	Mk 3:31-35 Lk 8:19-21	young woman with baby; "M"
Jesus	Lk 1:31-33 2:1-7	candle or lamp crib or manger; cross
Shepherds	Lk 2:8-20	shepherd's staff; lamb
Wise Men	Mt 2:1-12	gifts; star; camel
Simeon *and Anna*	Lk 2:22-38	old couple

The O Antiphons

These ancient and famous antiphons are described elsewhere in this volume. They mark the high point of the Advent liturgy and in our church receive a place of honour on the seven pillars surrounding the sanctuary.

The great O's were originally attached to the Magnificat and sung at vespers during the final week of Advent. Today in our new lectionary we find them as the gospel acclamations in Masses from 17th–24th December, when on each of these seven final days of Advent, with gathering momentum and expectancy the petitions are sung. We repeat the Antiphons here in order to suggest the appropriate symbol for each one.

1. O WISDOM (symbol: two-edged sword)

2. O ADONAI (symbol: sceptre)

3. O ROOT OF JESSE (symbol: flower on stem)

4. O KEY OF DAVID (symbol: key)

5. O RISING SUN (symbol: sun)

6. O KING (symbol: crown)

7. O EMMANUEL (manger)

Our church is a classical basilica-style church with 34 doric columns. In the final days of Advent the O Antiphon banners hang on the pillars around the sanctuary. Each new day is marked with the antiphon of the day, when the banner is removed from its pillar and receives a place of honour beside the Ambo from which the gospel acclamation and the Gospel of the day is proclaimed. This order has varied over the years. Once, we resurrected the old confraternity banners and gave them their old places around the church. This gave a festive effect and helped build up the expectancy, characteristic of this time.

Obviously, one has to take into consideration the lay-out of the church and the best possible ways to present visual aids to the greater advantage. It is important that the congregation knows what is going on and the why and the wherefore of each new symbol that appears.

The crib too should be built during Advent and adorned with only the straw, animals and the empty manger. This will speak volumes and will be thought-provoking for all making a serious preparation for the feast.

Basically we have taken the theme of the Advent liturgy. If our efforts are successful we thank God and feel amply rewarded that many people have come to a more thorough appreciation of what that liturgy is saying. If on the other hand it does not work, we learn from our mistakes and try again for next year.

These are modern ways and objects to visualise our faith and bring to life the stained-glass windows that are in most of our old churches. There will always be the need for change — just as the liturgy itself which is never static but alive — in order to speak to the modern day Christian.

John the Baptist was his Herald

Patrick Fitzgerald-Lombard, O Carm

"Prepare the way of the Lord": this is the great cry of Advent. This phrase catches the air of anticipation and expectancy which is the hallmark of the season. We know that Christ has come. We prepare to celebrate that coming with the sure hope that he will come again. Yet hope does not mean living in the future. It is rather a looking to the future while living in the present real world. Preparation of the way of the Lord must take place now, today. Advent is therefore the season of prophecy. A prophet is not one who foretells future events, although that meaning was common even at the time of our Lord. A prophet is primarily someone with a message from God for the people of his or her own generation. Certainly this message looks to a future fulfilment but that fulfilment demands immediate action by those who hear the message. Advent is a prophetic call for renewal as we await the coming of our Saviour.

"Prepare the way of the Lord": this is the great cry of John the Baptist. It is the phrase used by all four gospels to describe the ministry of John although only the Fourth Gospel puts it on the lips of John. Advent is the season which is dominated by the message of John the Baptist. His message was originally addressed to his contemporaries. It remains a message valid not only for us but for our contemporaries as well. The liturgy of Advent calls us to identify ourselves with John the Baptist.

All four gospel traditions about John the Baptist are represented in the Advent readings. The Fourth Gospel however is mentioned only briefly because its message belongs more to Christmas. By looking at all four gospel messages about

John we will get four different pictures of him. The three Synoptic Gospels while working with similar traditions use them to stress different aspects of John and his message. As always, it is important to remain close to the actual words of the gospels. The basis of our exploration will therefore be one passage from each gospel. This will allow us to see the meaning which John the Baptist brings to our Advent celebration.

The Beginning of the Gospel (Mk 1: 1-8)

It is fruitful to understand the Gospel of Mark from the end backwards. It is the resurrection which gives meaning to the passion which in turn gives meaning to the ministry. So the very first verse of the gospel is both a summary of the entire gospel and also a pointer to the ministry of John the Baptist. The gospel account itself is only a beginning, the good news itself will reach its final fulfilment only with the second coming of the Lord. At the same time, the beginning of that beginning is the ministry of John the Baptist.

Mark introduces John the Baptist with a composite quotation from the prophets Malachi (3:1) and Isaiah (40:3). The former in particular was linked with the return of the prophet Elijah before the last times. John the Baptist preached in the wilderness, the traditional place for purification (Is 41:16). He dressed like Elijah (2k 1:8). Yet Mark never says that John is Elijah. His concern is with the announcement of the last age.

Judea in 30AD was in a state of ferment. There was an eager expectation of a Messiah who would lead the Jews to victory over the Romans, the hated occupying power. A glorious future awaited the children of Abraham.

In a few words, Mark builds up a picture of excitement, the new age is about to dawn. It would however be very different to the one which had been expected. John the Baptist preached judgement for Israel. This is much clearer in the accounts of Matthew (3: 1-12) and Luke (3: 1-18). It seems that they have preserved John's own assessment of himself. Matthew and Luke give content to the message of John using the traditional prophetic image of winnowing (Is 4:4). John is preaching the coming of a powerful judge.

In Mark, John calls for repentance confirmed by the symbolic washing of a baptism. In verse 8 John makes the contrast between his baptism and the baptism of the mighty one who is coming (verse 7). The outpouring of the Holy Spirit was another sign of the last times (Jl 2: 28-29). Mark is here addressing himself to his own community who have experienced the outpouring of the Spirit by the Risen Lord. Already the Spirit will be present in the ministry of Jesus (1:10).

So already in this passage the contrast between John and Jesus is being made. The prologue of the gospel continues until verse 15. By this point the ministry of John is over and the ministry of Jesus is about to begin. The forerunner fades from the scene except for the surprisingly long account of his death in chapter 6. This death is foreshadowed in the prologue in verse 14. Advent concentrates on the ministry of John and his relationship to Jesus. The setting for this is that John like Jesus first preached and then was arrested or handed over and suffered and died. Already in Mark there is a hint of John as the prototype Christian disciple who must suffer like his Master.

The child in my womb leapt for joy (Lk 1 - 2)

The Holy Spirit also dominates the first two chapters of the Gospel of Luke. There is an outburst of prophetic activity leading to the joy of the last times (1: 14-15 or 1: 42, 44).

The birth narrative of Luke forms a closely constructed parallel between the births of John and Jesus. It is designed to show similarity between the two as well as the superiority of Jesus. The prologue anticipates the themes of the ministry, so already Luke has a meeting between John and Jesus. Even from the womb of his mother, John was filled with the Spirit of prophecy (1:15) and able with joy to recognise the Messiah (1:44). Already the ministries of John and Jesus begin to overlap.

Luke has a plan of history based on the three eras of the Time of Israel, the Time of Jesus and the Time of the Church. This scheme is not however rigid. John the Baptist forms a bridge between the Time of Israel and the Time of Jesus while the apostles form the bridge between the Time of Jesus and the Time of the Church. Luke sees a meaningful pattern in history, one which is based on continuity. The present situation is the fulfilment of the promises of the past while it also carries the promise of the future.

This becomes clear in the Canticle of Zechariah, the Benedictus (1: 68-79). The Benedictus is best described as a hymn of praise although its development is not as clear cut as, for example, Psalm 8. A hymn normally has an introduction and a conclusion with a body giving reasons for praise. Applying this to the Benedictus, the introduction is the first line of verse 68. The next line begins with "because"; the reason for praising God is the fulfilment of his promises first to David (68b to 71) and then to Abraham (72 to 75). This is the spirituality of the "poor ones", those who remained open to the promises of God. The next two verses (76 to 77) describe the mission of John the Baptist. They may be an addition to the canticle by Luke himself. Finally, the conclusion (78 to 79) refers to Jesus. He is the rising sun from on high (Is 60:1) who fulfils all the promises of the past and brings light into the new age. The Benedictus therefore shows a movement from the past to the future, from the Old Testament through John the Baptist to Jesus.

The emphasis of Luke is on John as the forerunner, the man who, like a colossus, has a foot in each age. He is the preparer of the way. He is firstly a prophet in the old style, "in the spirit and power of Elijah" (1:17). Verse 76 of the Benedictus reflects the Old Testament quotations Luke uses elsewhere (1:17; 3:4; 7:27). The parallels between John and Elijah are stressed less than in the other Synoptic Gospels.

Luke presents Jesus as a prophet and interprets him in terms of Elijah (4: 25-26).

John belongs also to the new age and so he is also shown as the first preacher of the Gospel. Verse 77 therefore uses Christian language. John will proclaim the knowledge or experience of salvation. In the ministry it is Luke alone who shows John giving precise instructions in response to a triple "what shall we do?" (3: 10, 12, 14). The birth of John is good news (1: 19), part of the Gospel.

Luke therefore uses the birth narrative to show the close relationship between John and Jesus which will be developed. Luke in fact makes the two blood relatives. John the Baptist has been brought into the Christian camp.

Blessed is he who takes no offence at me (Mt 11: 2-19)

Both Matthew and Luke record the visit to Jesus by the disciples of the imprisoned John and its sequel. Although the two accounts are very similar, the differences reflect the interests of the two evangelists. Luke omits the reference of Matthew to Elijah (Mt 11:14) and makes Jesus do healings in the presence of the messengers (Lk 7: 21).

For Matthew however, this scene is a seal on what has gone before. His gospel is carefully planned and the five great discourses are prominent. Chapters 11 and 12 lead from the discourse on discipleship in chapter 10 to the parables of chapter 13. The narrative is concerned with the conditions of belief and entry into the kingdom. The deeds of Christ (11: 2) refer to the Sermon on the Mount and the healings that followed (chapters 5-7 & 8-9).

There are three parts to the scene, each ending with a saying (verses 6, 15, 19). Overall, the scene is united by two references to deeds (verses 2 & 19).

The first part concerns Jesus more than John. John was a preacher of judgement and expected the traditional Day of the Lord (Am 5: 18-20). The Jesus who came was very different to these expectations. His mission was of healing and mercy rather than judgement and wrath. This part ends with a beatitude which calls upon John and the reader to be prepared to change their attitudes.

This theme of being open to the ways of God continues in the second part with an exhortation to hear at its end. It is about the identity of John but it leads to the identity of Jesus. The spirit of prophecy is abroad once more after a lapse of centuries. Yet it is time to go further. The kingdom of heaven is present in Jesus and a greater future awaits those who understand.

The final part shows just how hard it is to hear and understand. John and Jesus have both preached a similar message (3:2 & 4:17) in two very different ways. Neither satisfied the Jews and both were rejected. John stands for all who proclaim the Gospel, "this generation" (11: 16) applies to his own generation. Yet there will always be those who accept it (21: 32). Following on from the discourse of chapter 10, John becomes the first proclaimer of the Christian Gospel.

A Lamp, alight and shining (Jn 5: 33-36)

Chapter five of the Fourth Gospel develops from a healing on the Sabbath (5: 9). Jesus calls on witnesses to his claims (5: 31-40). Jewish Law required at least two witnesses for a condemnation (Dt 19: 15) although here the witnesses are to confirm the witness of Jesus. The first of these witnesses is John. However, Jesus immediately appeals to the higher witness of the works (miracles) granted him by the Father.

For the Fourth Gospel, the mission of John was to be a witness, a lamp and not the light (1: 8). John is no longer a prophet but a voice (1: 23). There may be an echo of a reference to Elijah in the image of a lamp (Sir 48: 1) but it is the voice from Isaiah which predominates. The message becomes more important than the messenger. John becomes a witness to Jesus as the Christ, a confessing Christian rather than an Old Testament prophet. He is a pointer towards Jesus and then fades from the scene. The evidence of the Fourth Gospel about John is therefore an appropriate exit point for the first part of Advent. The full message of this Gospel becomes important only after the great feast.

Prophets of the Most High

All four Gospels put a stress on John the Baptist fulfilling the prophecy from Isaiah and this may have been John's own assessment of his mission. He is linked with the expected messenger of the prophet Elijah; this may come from Jesus himself (Mt 17: 10-13). As the Church grew it claimed John the Baptist as its own. Many Christians probably came to Jesus through John (Jn 1: 37). So the gospels show John as a model Christian. The Church has always seen in John a means of setting out its own part in the preparation of the way of the Lord. John the Baptist is an image of the Church as a herald, proclaiming the good news of Jesus to the world.

The Benedictus shows us the foundation for being heralds of the Lord. Our hope for the future, the good news which we proclaim, receives its conviction because we know that God has fulfilled his promises in the past. Our Advent liturgy reminds us that the yearning of Judaism for the Day of the Lord has already happened in Jesus Christ. We still yearn for the second coming of the Lord in glory. Advent allows us to pray for greater strength as we prepare for the Second Advent.

This is the setting for John the Baptist, the prophet. As a prophet John was courageously able to speak the word of God to the people of his generation. He was not part of the system of government (Mt 11: 8). On the contrary, he kept independent of it and was prepared to denounce its excesses. This resulted in his arrest and execution. John the Baptist calls us to work for social justice in our world today. We have to be prepared to stand back from human institutions. We have to be prepared to suffer. For this, we must go into the wilderness in order to see clearly the message, the values of the good news.

Even so, what will happen will be unexpected. John had to change his attitudes because the Messiah who came was not what he anticipated (Mt 11: 2). Our preparation for the Second Advent requires the ability to listen and to be open. In many languages, "obedience" and "hearing" are similar words. To hear is to obey. We talk about obeying the will of God yet it is all too easy to settle down and become fixed in our ways. The word of God will always challenge us because it will be fulfilled in ways that we do not expect.

John the Baptist was the herald of the final age. His birth and his ministry came with joy and with the outpouring of the Holy Spirit. We have received the Baptism of the Holy Spirit (Mk 1: 8) given to us by the risen Lord. This makes us more than prophets, we become witnesses to Christ. Our mission as heralds is to point to Christ, to make him known when he comes (Advent preface). We are lamps reflecting the light of Christ. In this way the Church becomes a beacon of hope for the whole world.

The Liturgy of the Sundays of Advent

Brian Magee CM

"Advent has a twofold character; as a season to prepare for Christmas when Christ's first coming to us is remembered; as a season when that remembrance directs the mind and heart to await Christ's Second Coming at the end of time. Advent is thus a period for devout and joyful expectation." *General Norms for the Liturgical Year, no. 39.*

The stress is not on a season of penance in preparation for Christmas or even final judgement; it is part of the festive celebration of Christmas, and as a consequence an expectation in hope and joy of the parousia. This preparation for Christmas is especially highlighted in the period from December 17 to December 24.

The liturgy can only celebrate the events that are historical as they are the memorial of the actions of God in our lives. But we cannot celebrate the events that we await, such as Christ's coming in judgement and the realisation of the Kingdom. So in the first part of Advent the remembrance of the events of the incarnation are not excluded since it is on the basis of these that we look forward to the second coming.

The proper texts of the three year cycle in the Roman Missal are the same for each year.

There is a three year cycle of readings in the lectionary for Mass, years A, B and C.

First Sunday of Advent

For the past few Sundays the readings have pointed to the last judgement, the end of the world, the general judgement and the new heaven and new earth. We begin the season of

Advent with a sort of conclusion to all this. The First Sunday is still about the last things, but in a spirit of joy and hope. There is a call to be ready for these things to happen soon. So the idea of vigilance as we wait for the Lord comes to the front. This waiting is not characterised by fear but rather by thanksgiving and hope.

Year A

First Reading Isaiah 2:1-5
The Lord gathers all the nations together into the eternal peace of God's kingdom.

We are shown a vision of what the end of the world will be like. Our first thoughts are not of fear or dread of the future, but of peace among nations that have come together in unity through obedience to God's law! It is a vision that all people would like to see fulfilled. And indeed, the words of Isaiah are written on the United Nations building in New York.

Responsorial Psalm Ps 121

The vision of all the peoples together with the Lord in peace is continued in the psalm.

Second Reading Romans 13:11-14
Our Salvation is near.

The first reading ended with the exhortation to walk in the light. St Paul takes up that same theme and reminds us that the day is at hand so we must live in the daylight. So today we have already that ancient Christmas theme of light in darkness, the conquering Sun that shatters the night. And Paul makes that practical by calling on Christians not to abuse sex, drink or relationships.

Gospel Matthew 24:37-44
Stay awake that you may be ready.

This passage brings us again face to face with the end times. We have the warning of Jesus that it will come with disturbing unexpectedness. His call is to stay awake, another variant of being in the light.

Homily directions

Todays's liturgy then is bringing together ideas in a conclusion, and at the same time is making a new beginning. The warnings of the final Sundays of Ordinary Time are summarised in a call to watchfulness, in good Christian living, in joyful hope for the final peace. The first Sunday of this new season encourages us to look forward with expectation to the coming of Christ.

This looking forward fits in with the sense of the nearness of Christmas, the number of shopping days left, the lighting up of shopping areas, and the feeling that December is not too bad a month despite the darkness and weather.

But the liturgy calls for a looking forward, preparing now by putting aside sin and evil habits, by increasing "our strength of will for doing good, and setting our hearts on heaven."

Year B

First Reading Isaiah 63:16b-17,64:1,3b-8
Oh, that you would tear the heavens open and come down.

This passage gives the text for the Latin hymn *Rorate caeli desuper,* which once characterised this season so well. It is a confession of failure and sinfulness on our part, but it is not a cry of despair. It expresses hope that God would tear open the heavens and come to us. We do not fear that coming for he is our Father, we the work of his hands, like vessels made by the potter.

Responsorial Psalm Psalm 80

The psalm responds in the same way with a call for God to come, to shine from his throne. He is the shepherd who will lead us, he is the vinedresser who encourages growth.

Second Reading 1 Corinthians 1:3-9
We are waiting for our Lord Jesus Christ to be revealed.

St Paul reminds the community that all their gifts from God are not to make them careless. They have still to be vigilant in their waiting for the coming of the Lord. They need to have the gift of final perseverance, with clear consciences when he does come.

Gospel Mark 13:33-37
Stay awake, because you do not known when the master of the house is coming.

There is a warning to be vigilant. Three times in this short passage comes the command, "stay awake". The parable is about those who are looking after the house in the absence of the owner, and who are to be ready to let him in on his return – whenever that might be.

Homily directions

The readings today are saying many things to the Church community, and perhaps to each local community. There is an acknowledgement that all may not be well with the way the Church is living. There is a warning against complacency, taking God's gifts for granted. And there is a call to greater watchfulness in living the Christian way. There is also the encouragement that God is himself watchful for his people. He is the careful potter, the loving father, the good shepherd, the faithful one.

Year C

First Reading Jeremiah 33:14-16
I will make a virtuous branch grow for David.

This oracle of Jeremiah, revived from Ch 23, is spoken to a people who have begun to despair of God's promise and are returning to other gods. Its promise is fulfilled in Christ.

Responsorial Psalm Psalm 24

The psalm picks up the theme of God's integrity spoken of by Jeremiah. It speaks of patient waiting for the Lord's coming.

Second Reading 1 Thessalonians 3:12-42
May the Lord confirm your hearts in holiness when Christ comes.

St Paul prays that this community will continue to grow until the coming of the Lord. Their growth in holiness will

42

be based on their knowledge of Christ through the tradition handed on and from their own experience of him.

Gospel Luke 21:25-28,34-36
Your liberation is near at hand.

The Church which is now part of the human world is directed to keep its gaze fixed on the coming of the Son of God in judgement. There is to be no slackening, no slipping into lax ways.

Homily directions

Both Jeremiah and Luke speak to communities that are tempted to tire in their waiting in hope. The temptation is to make the most of the life around them and neglect the true God. Our prayer after communion prays that we may keep our gaze on heaven as we make our way through this life. Yet this must not narrow us to aiming at personal salvation alone, but rather make us work more earnestly for the building of God's kingdom here in our social situation.

Second Sunday of Advent

On this Sunday the liturgy moves on from the apocalyptic theme towards Christ's coming in history and sacramentally at Christmas. Every time we celebrate the liturgy we celebrate the good news that Jesus Christ has died for us and is risen in glory. On this day we are asked to enter into that mystery through conversion. The figure of John the Baptist appears preparing the way. His call is to repentance.

Year A

First Reading Isaiah 11:1-10
He judges the wretched with integrity.

This passage points to Christ. It was an idealised portrait of the king that Israel desired. It is realised in Jesus. He is the one gifted with intelligence, ability and holiness. As we look towards Christmas we recognise in him the little child that will lead us.

Responsorial Psalm 71

This psalm repeats the qualifications of the king, one full of wisdom, able to act for the poor, and favoured by God.

Second Reading Romans 15:4-9
Christ is the Saviour of all.

St Paul stresses that the events of the Old Testament are there to encourage our hope. In the wonderful works of God in the past we see his power available to us now. The coming of Christ has given us the power to live as he did, and to be one in love with all.

Gospel Matthew 3:1-12
Repent, for the kingdom of heaven is close at hand.

John the Baptist reminds us that we cannot claim exemption because we are baptised disciples of Christ. Penance and conversion are continuing processes in our lives. His words were first addressed to those who claimed privilege because Abraham was their father. Now they are directed to all who claim Jesus as their saviour.

Homily directions

The opening prayer asks that God "remove the things that hinder us from receiving Christ with joy". And the tough words of John the Baptist call us to repentance. Part of our preparation for Christmas is to celebrate reconciliation, to ready ourselves to meet Christ with right conscience. The celebration of the sacrament of reconciliation has a prominent place in Advent preparation. We are called to this penance by the model of Jesus. His human image is highlighted in our readings, he is a signal to the peoples. He is a sign of hope in the mind of St Paul. People who do not give up, he reminds us, are helped by God. No one can be held back from the kindness of Christ who acted in a friendly way. Coming to be like him in wisdom and piety we can, in the words of the final prayer, learn "to judge wisely the things of earth and to love the things of heaven."

Year B

First Reading Isaiah 40:1-5,9-11
Prepare a way for the Lord.

This is one of the most familiar passages in the prophecies of Isaiah. Various parts have been set to music and are familiar to many people today. The original meaning of the passage was one of hope for the return of the people of Israel to their own kingdom after the Babylonian exile. It is an expression of trust through remembrance. The recalling of God's mighty works at the Exodus gives encouragement that he will do them again in this time. It is the hope that he who parted the waters will level the mountains. The final verses in this reading bring forward the image of Christ, the Good Shepherd, calling us to himself with love.

Responsorial Psalm Psalm 85

The psalm continues this hope for God to continue his great works in history. It envisages the new kingdom of justice, peace and fruitfulness.

Second Reading 2 Peter 3:8-14
We are waiting for the new heaven and new earth.

Christians came gradually to recognise that the second coming was not to be as soon as they had once expected. In this letter that realisation has already begun. The author is reminding us all that it is not how soon it may be that is important, but rather how sudden it may be. Time with God is not measured as we measure it. Christians in every age are to be watchful and ready, to live as if the end were today. This leads to a striving for holiness of life.

Gospel Mark 1:1-8
Make his paths straight.

John the Baptist is seen preaching with the words of the prophet Isaiah given in our first reading. He is seen as the messenger in the prophecy of Malachi. His message is two-fold, a call to conversion and a pointing to one who is to come. His baptism is a sign of repentance that leads to a confession of sins.

Homily directions

The readings together call us to holiness of life as our way of celebrating Christmas. John the Baptist speaks to each one of us today as he did to those who came to the Jordan. We have to straighten out our lives, lower the mountains of pride so that God's grace can lead us to do what he wants with us. St Peter's new heaven and new earth has no place for our selfishness and pride. We cannot put off the day for repentance but must get down to it now. Are we able to say the opening prayer of today that the lure of greed may not impede us from the joy which moves the hearts of those who seek Christ?

Year C

First Reading Baruch 5:1-9
God means to show your splendour to every nation.

The journey of the Christian people is not an easy one. But this prophecy encourages us along the way. We see the Church in its final shape, dressed as it were to meet God. It is what we are called to be. So let us stand on the heights and look eastwards in expectation of the Lord!

Responsorial psalm Psalm 125

The sense of joy in expectation is brought out by this song, one of the psalter's most beautiful expressions of hope. The sense of waiting for the harvest, and the joy of gathering it in echoes St James' farmer who waits patiently.

Second Reading Philippians 1:4-6, 8-11
Be pure and blameless for the day of Christ.

St Paul recognises the difficulties of his Christians in facing the temptations of this world. He prays that they may overcome all things through love. Their practice of Christian love will lead them to new understandings, so that they will know what is best for each situation. In that way they will have arrived at maturity when Christ comes.

Gospel Luke 3:1-6
All shall see the salvation of God.

St Luke sees John the Baptist as the last of the Old Testament prophets who tells of the imminent coming of the Messiah. After him begins the period of Jesus, first in his earthly life, and then, in Acts, as his presence through the Church.

Homily directions

These readings bring a sense of expectation to our Advent progress. We are to look forward with joy. And yet there is still some hesitation, some fear of the future. There is much work to be done in making a new world for Christ, new roads to be built. We cannot do it by ourselves. The incarnation and the parousia speak to us of God's intervention in our history, without which we can make a mess of the world.

Third Sunday of Advent

The former title of this Sunday was *Gaudete Sunday* from the first word of the entrance song, *Rejoice*. It was a copy of the *Laetare Sunday* of mid Lent. The idea of highlighting a theme of joy fits the mood of Advent. The first readings particularly sound the note, with the psalm, such as the Magnificat, following on. The second reading shows how joy comes into the Christian life. It is a joy that is firmly based. John the Baptist is with us still in the Gospel, showing us how to prepare for the coming of Christ as we move towards the preparation for Christmas.

Year A

First Reading Isaiah 35:1-6,10
God himself is coming to save you.

This passage is quoted in the Gospel today, where it is seen as being about Christ, the one who is to come. We rejoice at the news of God's coming. Christ who healed the blind and the deaf, and raised up the crippled is the cause of our joy.

Responsorial Psalm Psalm 145

The response expresses our trust in Christ who looks after the poor and needy. It is through him that the reign of God is established.

Second Reading James 5:7-10
Do not lose heart, for the Lord's coming will be soon.

Again we are directed to the future. If our Advent waiting seems long we are encouraged to patience. But James points us even further to another look at the final judgement. We are to live in patience and love which are part of hope. And like all the people of the Old Testament we are not to give up that hope.

Gospel Matthew 11:2-11
Are you the one who is to come, or have we got to wait for someone else?

The question in the Gospel today, "Are you the one who is to come?" is also our question. We too are called to recognise Jesus. He himself gives an answer to the question when he asks us to see the signs of God's power in all those who have been healed. John sent his disciples to meet Jesus that they might have faith in him. John is praised for his strength and faithfulness.

Homily directions

We take for granted the appearance of John the Baptist preaching preparation for Christmas in the Advent liturgy. Yet he did not come before the birth of Christ, but before his public ministry. We celebrate at Christmas the incarnation, which is the whole event of Christ's coming among us as the love of God. The nativity is a part of that so John can take his place in our liturgical memorial of that event. His function is to point out Jesus to us. The figure that appears on these Advent Sundays is the mature Christ who is seen in his healing ministry. Since so much of the popular approach to Christmas is in terms of the *Baby Jesus* it is useful to present this portrait beforehand. The Christ we celebrate at Christmas is the one who has died for us, is risen and is to come as our judge.

First Reading Isaiah 61:1-2,10-11
I exult for joy in the Lord.
These words of Isaiah are used by the evangelists as applying to Jesus. They are his own understanding of his mission. The coming of a man of such integrity calls for rejoicing.

Responsorial Psalm Luke 1:46-50, 53-54 *Magnificat*
The song of Mary echoes the cry of joy in the reading and is filled with the spirit of Advent waiting.

Second Reading 1 Thessalonians 5:16-24
May you all be kept safe, spirit, soul and body, for the coming of the Lord.
The call to joy opens this passage. The Christian community is to be distinguished by joy, prayer and thanksgiving. These virtues come from an obedience to the Holy Spirit. This will enable each one to grow and develop with discernment. And again the Christian is one who waits in joyful hope. The theme of the parousia is not lost even so near to Christmas.

Gospel John 1:6-8,19-28
There stands among you — unknown to you — the one who is coming after me.
As we do later in the year we use St John's Gospel today to make up for the shorter length of St Mark. But the reading is made up of two extracts about John the Baptist. It is the later understanding of John as one who prepared the way for Christ, and had no claims himself to be the Messiah. He points to Christ as the true Messiah.

Homily directions
"Anticipation is better than realisation" the saying goes. There is a kind of waiting that is enjoyable, just as there is a waiting that is full of anguish. Waiting in joy is what Advent

is about. Today the anticipation of the coming of Christ is highlighted in the Gospel. How we live out that waiting in a spirit of Christian joy is spelled out in the other readings. These call for openness to the Spirit, and a sense of justice and peace in daily living.

Year C

First Reading Zephaniah 3:14-18a
The Lord will dance with shouts of joy for you as on a day of festival.

What a marvellous invitation to rejoice today is found in this passage! It demands a liturgy in which singing and dancing have their place. There is a strong reminder for us of the difference the intervention of God in our lives makes.

Responsorial Psalm Isaiah 12:26

We use the first song of Isaiah today to thank God for salvation in Christ, who lives ever among his people.

Second Reading Philippians 4:4-7
The Lord is very near.

This was the traditional reading that gave the name *Gaudete* to this Sunday. Prayer and thanksgiving lead the Christian to be at peace throughout all life's ups and downs.

Gospel Luke 3:10-18
What must we do?

There are two themes in this passage; firstly, John's message to the people on how to live, and then his clarification of his role as the one who points to the real Messiah.

Homily directions

Christians should be people of joy. But many see their religious life as one in which fear and trembling have too large a part. Peace and serenity come from knowing God's will and doing it. John tells the people what to do, and his advice is to be just, in whatever situation or vocation they find themselves. His knowledge of his own vocation to ser-

50

vice reminds us that Christians are like John and Christ called to serve and not to be served.

Fourth Sunday of Advent

This Sunday falls within the second period of Advent, that of immediate preparation for the Christmas festival. Mary becomes the key figure in the Gospel. The account of the Annunciation and the role of Mary in the economy of salvation bring us right up against the mystery of the incarnation that we celebrate at Christmas.

Year A

First Reading Isaiah 7:10-14
The maiden is with child.

The sign that Isaiah offers of the young maiden bearing a son is one of promise and hope for the line of king David. This hope finds its fulfilment for Christians in Jesus Christ who is of that line of David. The sign is used in the Gospel passage for today.

Responsorial Psalm Psalm 23

This is a hymn of expectation for the One who is to come, and at the same time a call to be prepared for his coming, with clean hands and pure heart.

Second Reading Romans 1: 1-7
Jesus Christ, descendant of David, Son of God.

Paul shows himself a preacher of the good news about Jesus Christ, who in his human nature was descended from David, and who through the paschal mystery is enthroned as Son of God. The incarnation is seen today as part of that paschal mystery we celebrate on each Sunday.

Gospel Matthew 1:18-24
Jesus is born of Mary who was betrothed to Joseph, son of David.

The mystery of the Incarnation is about the intervention of God in human history. Yet the story in today's Gospel is about ordinary people living out what seems a very human

51

situation. In that story we are told that Jesus is of the messianic line of David, that the Holy Spirit played an important role in the event, and that Jesus came to save us from our sins.

Homily directions

The Sunday before Christmas is an important moment to draw attention to the true meaning of the feast before it is lost in the accidentals of the day itself. In the light of the resurrection of Christ we see the meaning of the story we are remembering. The child whose birth we celebrate is the Saviour of the world, he is the Lord. He is the one who by his human and divine natures links heaven and earth, is the one Mediator. Through him we have access to the throne of grace. That is the reason for our festivity, not nostalgia about a lovely story in the past, or family togetherness, or whatever other understanding has attached itself to Christmas.

Year B
First Reading 2 Samuel 7:1-5,8-12,14,16
The kingdom of David will always stand secure before the Lord.

The promise of the throne to David mentioned in the Gospel by the angel is here given as Nathan brings God's message. The promise of an everlasting House of David finds fulfilment in Jesus Christ, of the House of David.

Responsorial Psalm Psalm 88

The faithfulness of the Lord to his promises, and particularly to the promise to David is the burden of this song.

Second Reading Romans 16:25-27
The Mystery, which was kept secret for endless ages, is now made clear.

The meaning of the story of our salvation as seen in the Old Testament is only understood fully in the light of Christ. These verses of praise rejoice in the knowledge of that mystery now clearly revealed.

52

Gospel Luke 1:26-38
Listen! You are to conceive and bear a son.

This most familiar story is one of faith. It is presented in a literary form common to such events in the Sacred Scripture. The purpose is to explain to us who Jesus Christ is, the role of Mary, the choice of God, the work of the Holy Spirit. Like a good story it is simple and yet full of depths. Before it we can make our act of faith.

Homily directions

The spirit of waiting of Advent should not be ended by anticipating the Christmas theme of incarnation. Today is about the preparations for that event. Mary herself and her vocation to be the Mother of God — so well presented in the letter of Pope Paul VI *Marialis Cultus* — will obviously be the main interest. But also the whole story of revelation through Christ in word and sacrament, and the call to be apostles of that mystery can be presented.

Year C

First Reading Micah 5:2-5a
Out of you, Bethlehem, will be born the one who is to rule over Israel.

Micah speaks to the hopes for the restoration of the Davidic monarchy at the end of the exile. These hopes are seen by Christians as being fulfilled in Christ, the Good Shepherd. The very name of Bethlehem brings us closer to our celebration of Christmas.

Responsorial psalm Psalm 79

This psalm gives particular expression to the prayer of Advent. It appeals to the Shepherd of Israel for help.

Second Reading Hebrews 10:5-10
Here I am! I am coming to do your will.

This passage shows how at Christmas we are still celebrating the Paschal Mystery. It is the Incarnate Word who gives himself up for us and whose sacrifice is accepted by the Father.

Gospel Luke 1:39-45
Why should I be honoured with a visit from the mother of my Lord?

The Gospel speaks of Mary as she visits Elizabeth. In her time of waiting she still makes room in love for Elizabeth in her joy too.

Homily directions

Mary is called "blessed" three times in the Gospel, for her faith and obedience and for carrying the Christ child. Her blessedness comes from her relationship with Christ as one graced by God. That faith and obedience will be put to the test and will be seen on Calvary when Christ himself gives the example of perfect obedience to the Father — "I come to do your will". As we prepare for Christmas, and indeed in all our life of waiting for the Lord, acts of Christian charity should characterise us.

Music for Advent

Jeremiah Threadgold

Advent is about the coming of the Lord — past, present and future, or in history, in mystery and in glory. There is a great variety of themes in the Advent liturgy. Isaiah can tell us to "make straight a highway for our God". The Baptist can advise us to "repent, for the kingdom of God is at hand" and the gospels remind us to "stay awake, because you do not know the day when the master will come". On the other hand Zephaniah reminds us to "shout for joy. The Lord is in your midst" and Saint Paul says "I want you to be happy always, happy in the Lord". This variety of themes is reflected in the vast amount of music which is suitable for the season.

It should be obvious that Christmas music should be reserved for the Christmas season and Advent music should be sung during Advent. But in fact there are many carol services during Advent — both in schools and in parishes — not to mention carol singers and shopping centre hype. Liturgically this is not right, and psychologically too — for we tire of the Christmas carols long before Christmas comes.

Would it not be lovely to hear Silent Night sung for the first time when the infant figure is laid in the manger at Midnight Mass? Then we would be celebrating the fulfilment of all our Advent prayers and songs.

The alive parish will want music for each of the Sunday Masses, and perhaps weekly services, based on the Prayer of the Church or biblical themes. The great personalities of Isaiah, John the Baptist and Mary will be foremost in song and prayer and a highpoint of Advent worship could be a service or even a seven day novena (17-23rd December) built around the O Antiphons. A parish might celebrate a communal service of reconciliation too in preparation for Christmas.

Music Resources for Advent

Not only have we many fine hymnals with traditional material, but in recent years many new resources have appeared. The Spirit is truly alive in the Church and composers have widely experienced the creative charism.

Let's look first at some of the most popular hymnals in current use.

On the eastern side of the Atlantic *Praise the Lord* is a fine hymnal published by Chapman in 1971. All the well-known Advent hymns are there (124-137). Another excellent book is *With One Voice* published by Collins in 1979. Not only is there a comprehensive Advent section but the scriptural index provides useful references to settings of Isaiah, the Baptist and Mary. Veritas published the *Veritas Hymnal* in 1973 and *Alleluia Amen* in 1978. They have good Advent sections with a certain amount of repetition and a share of originals.

Two other English publications deserve special mention. *Music for the Mass* edited by Geoffrey Boulton Smith, and published by Chapman in 1985 contains some interesting original material. Have a look at *Come to set us free* by Bernadette Farrell. The Thomas More Centre for Pastoral Liturgy published *He Comes To Set Us Free* in 1982. This is an outstandng resource. I particularly like the Advent/Christmas litany by Paul Inwood

Coming from France there is the music of Lucien Deiss, with many good Advent songs including *Holy Mother of our Redeemer* which is a translation of the Marian Anthem *Alma Redemptoris Mater, (Biblical Hymns and Psalms,* 2 volumes and *Sing for the Lord,* published by World Library). Margaret Daly includes some of the fine Lourdes music by Decha and Lecot in her two volumes of *Alleluia Amen.* Note

Let us welcome the Lord (AA105) and *Renew your hearts* (AA77).

Then there is the extraordinary music of *Taizé,* with Advent sections in Vol I and Vol II published by Collins. *Wait for the Lord* (Vol II p78) is a fine ostinato response with many verses taken from the classical texts. In Vol 1 there are two good settings of *Maranatha* in the form of acclamations.

From the United States there are two outstanding resources. *Worship II* published by the GIA, Chicago, is rich in Advent material (index 12) and *The ICEL Resource Collection* published by GIA in 1981, (liturgical index 8 and scriptural index 23) is particularly useful.

Then there is the folk repertoire. First you should look at the *Glory and Praise, Leader's Guide* published by NALR in 1983. This is an analysis of the 3 volumes *Glory and Praise* and contains many excellent hymns for the Sundays of Advent and a scriptural index which is very far reaching. Two books which deserve special mention are *We Have Seen His Star* (World Library 1981) and *Gentle Night* (NALR 1979), another success from the Saint Louis Jesuits.

There are also the many volumes published by Saint Meinrad Archabbey and Weston Priory. From Weston look at *Go up to the Mountain* (Isaiah 38 and 40), *Locusts and Wild Honey* (The Baptist), *Come back to me* (Hosea) and the *Prophet's cry* (Isaiah).

The Old Latin classics should not be ignored. I have already mentioned the *Alma Redemptoris Mater.* The *Rorate Caeli Desuper* and the *Creator Alme Siderum* should also be mentioned.

Mary is the greatest Advent figure. Every hymnal has a comprehensive Marian section — check the seasonal and scriptural indexes. In particular the Basque carol *The angel Gabriel to Mary came (Praise the Lord* 137) and *A message came to a Maiden Young (Worship II)* of Dutch origin, are both rewarding. Naturally her own canticles, the *Benedictus* and the *Magnificat* are basic.

Breviary Hymns for Advent

There are four hymns printed in the Advent Section. A word about tunes and accompaniments.

1. Hear the Herald Voice Resounding
   Tune: Merton *(Praise the Lord 132)*
          St Columba *(Veritas 83)*

2. Creator of the Stars of Night
   Tune: Creator Alme Siderum *(Praise the Lord 125)*
          Suantraí *(Veritas 25)*

3. The Co-Eternal Son
   Tune: Optatus *(Praise the Lord 134)*

4. O Come, O Come Emmanuel
   Tune: Veni Emmanuel *(Praise the Lord 131)*
          (Veritas 60)

Psalms for Advent

It is quite simple to go to a source book for settings of the Psalms of Advent. Fintan O'Carroll's *Responsorial Psalms for Sundays and Feasts* (ICMA 1983) contains settings for all the psalms of the 3 year cycle. Similarly, Geoffrey Boulton Smith's *A Responsorial Psalm Book* (Collins 1979) covers the same ground — perhaps with more variety because he has a team of well-known composers. For folk settings *Glory and Praise* (Leader's Guide) gives a comprehensive list of psalms.

Perhaps the most imaginative approach is Lucien Deiss' *Alleluia, Sing with New Songs* (World Library 1981). Here we find psalms and gospel acclamations for all the Sundays and Holy Days of Advent/Christmas. There are alternative settings too, simple and ornate. Some of these songs have already become firm favourites like the round *Alleluia, he sent me forth* (4) and the previously mentioned *Incantation* (6).

The O Antiphons

The O Antiphons are the alleluia verses of the Mass and the Magnificat antiphons of Evening Prayer for the seven days preceeding the vigil of Christmas. Each in its own unique way expresses the great God and saviour Jesus Christ who is about to enter human history. Christ of the O Antiphons is the Christ of John's Gospel — 'The word was God, and the word became flesh, and dwelt amongst us, and we have seen his glory'. This rather than the helpless babe of Luke or Saint Francis of Assisi. Composed by some anonymous person probably in the 9th century, they are all directly culled from the scriptures, old and new testament. They start with a divine title — O Emmanuel etc. They continue with a statement of his greatness and his will to save, and end with a prayer or invocation for deliverance.

Primarily they are used for Mass and Evening Prayer. They could be used for family prayer in preparation for Christmas. It would also be possible to devise a short prayer service each day, with hymns, readings and prayers, built around the antiphon of the day.

Or perhaps it would be good to have one big Advent evening in Church with a service devised around the seven antiphons, with readings and prayers, perhaps a seven branch candlestick on the altar, a new candle lit for each antiphon. There could be seven banners too, each with images evoked by the antiphons. A darkened church with emphasis on the banners and a light in front of each help to create a prayerful mood of anticipation.

Music for the O Antiphons

The best known setting is the seven verse hymn, *O Come, O Come, Emmanuel*. Each verse represents an antiphon. Lucien Deiss has a fine setting in *Heavens drop dew from above (Biblical hymns and Psalms* Vol I no. 2). For a folk setting the monks of Weston Priory give seven settings in *Go up to the Mountain*. Deiss has another lovely setting of four of the Antiphons in *Incantation for the Coming of Christ (Alleluia, Sing with New Songs* No. 6) but they really have to be sung together as a unit. Finally, Veritas Publications have *The O Antiphons* (1979) with two excellent settings of all the antiphons by Seoirse Bodley and Gerard

Victory. In these settings there are attractive cantor lines, very simple choral harmonies and basic yet fine congregational responses. They have proved their excellence over the years. The liturgical notes by Brian Magee are a great help if you are arranging an Advent service.

Sundays in Advent

If there is to be good participation in the music at Sunday Masses there should be a limited repertoire. If there are too many changes the people will lose heart and volume in similar proportions. On the other hand, choirs and folk groups will seek variety.

Choirs will find *Carols for Choirs* (O.U.P. Vol II) of special interest, with choral settings for Advent. They vary in difficulty from the lovely *Zion hears the Watchmen's Voices* (Bach, Cantata 140) to *Veni Emmanuel* arranged by David Willcocks.

I give finally a very personal choice of music for the Sundays, based strictly on the readings of the occasion and chosen from only three or four sources. The fact that all themes could so easily be covered is an indication of the huge repertoire of music now available.

May the gift of music and your dedication bring about the fulfilment of God's kingdom. *Veni Domine, et none tardare.*

SOME MUSIC FOR SUNDAY MASSES

Sunday 1
Waiting for the Lord (Isaiah)

YEAR A
The Nations Gather (Isaiah 2)
1. A time will come for singing
   Schutte
   Gentle Night 38
   or

Personal Choice

2. Behold the Mountain of the
   Lord
   ICEL Resource Collection 1981

YEAR B
May God come down (Isaiah 63)
1. Redeemer Lord
   Foley
   Glory and Praise 23

YEAR C
A Just Shoot (Jeremiah 33)
   Come O Lord
   Damaens 10

Sunday 2
Prepare the Way of the Lord
(John the Baptist)

YEAR A
*The Spirit of the Lord is upon
him* (Isaiah 11)
   Son of David
   Foley
   Glory and Praise 145

YEAR B
Fill in the Valley (Isaiah 40)
1. O Comfort my People
   Veritas Hymnal 63
2. Let the Valleys be raised
   Schutte
   Gentle Night 28
3. Take Comfort
   ICEL 25

YEAR C
Every mountain laid low
(Baruch 5)
    Arise Jerusalem
    Alleluia Amen 10

Sunday 3
The Coming Messiah (John the
Baptist)

YEAR A
Healing: Signs of his coming
(Isaiah 35)
1. Let the dry land sing
    Middleton
    We have seen his star 24
2. Patience People
    Foley
    Gentle Night 32

YEAR B
Good news to the Poor
(Isaiah 61)
1. Hark the Glad Sound
    ICEL 5
2. Lay your hands
    Landry
    Glory and Praise 32
3. Come thou long expected Jesus
    ICEL 2

YEAR C
Rejoice! God is in your midst
(Zephaniah 3)
1. And the Father will dance
    Landry
    Glory and Praise 4

2. Rejoice the Lord is King
   ICEL 108

Sunday 4
The Incarnation

YEAR A
A Virgin Shall conceive (Isaiah 7)
1. *O Come, O Come, Emmanuel*
   (Passim)
2. Who has known
   Foley
   Gentle Night 42

YEAR B
Your house forever before me
(2 Samuel)
1. A Dwelling Place
   Foley
   Glory and Praise 12
2. Pange Lingua (Verse 2) Latin
   or English.

YEAR C
She who is to give birth (Micah 5)
1. O Little Town of Bethlehem
   (Passim)
2. Lord Today
   Damaens
   Glory and Praise 118
3. Praised be the Flower
   Deiss
   Glory and Praise 230

The O Antiphons

Brian Magee CM

Our readings and hymns in Advent use mainly the words of Old Testament prophets expressing a longing for the saviour to come. The final days of the season accentuate that longing, and find its expression most beautifully in the great vesper antiphons for the Magnificat, called "The O Antiphons" because they being with the interjection O.

They are thought to have been composed in the 8th century by some anonymous cantor, and achieved great popularity in the Middle Ages. Great solemnity attended their intonation in the monasteries. They were sung in the solemn tone of great feasts, the great bell of the abbey was tolled, and, beginning with the abbot, they were intoned by the chief office holders of the monastery.

The O Antiphons are still used at the Magnificat in Evening Prayer of the Church, and also as the gospel acclamation in the Masses of these days so making them more accessible to the general faithful. They should, of course, be sung.*

These antiphons are mosaics of scripture texts expressing a longing for salvation and liberation. As many prophets and wise men longed to see the day of Christ so we can express our longing for his coming in these words. We use their words in a totally contemporary way, it is our prayer today for salvation. In the words of Adrian Nocent OSB, "These antiphons express the theology of Advent and are the season's brightest jewels."

*Music for the antiphons to be used at Evening Prayer or the gospel acclamation has been composed by Seoirse Bodley and Gerard Victory and is published by Veritas Publications, Ireland.

17 December

O Sapientia, quae ex ore Altissimi prodisti, attingens a fine usque ad finem, fortiter suaviter disponensque omnia: veni ad docendum nos viam prudentiae.

O Wisdom, O holy Word of God, you govern all creation with your strong yet tender care. Come and show your people the way to salvation. (ICEL)

O Wisdom, you come forth from the mouth of the Most High. You will the universe and hold all things together in a strong yet gentle manner. O come to teach us the way of truth. (Divine Office)

Sirach 24:3 Wisdom 8:1 Isaiah 40:3-4

This ancient antiphon is sung on the first day of our deeper preparation for Christmas and Epiphany. We pray to know the right way. The right way to live as Christians, the right way to celebrate Christmas, the right way to live these days of preparation. Advent prayers at Mass call us to remembrance of priorities in the gift of life. We ask to be taught how to judge wisely the things of earth and to love the things of heaven. "Teach us to live by your wisdom", we pray. It is true wisdom to know where our real treasure is hidden.

18 December

O Adonai, et Dux domus Israel, qui Moysi in igne flammae rubi apparuisti, et ei in Sina Legem dedisti: veni ad redimendum nos in brachio extento.

O sacred Lord of ancient Israel, who showed yourself to Moses in the burning bush, who gave him the holy way on Sinai mountain; come, stretch out your mighty hand to set us free. (ICEL)

O Adonai and leader of Israel, you appeared to Moses in a burning bush and you gave him the law on Sinai. O come and save us with your mighty power. (Divine Office)

Exodus 6:2,3,12 Exodus 3:2 Exodus 6:6

At the burning bush Moses came to know the name of the Lord God.

Knowing someone's name is to bring that person closer to us. Indeed in many cultures it meant having power over them. God in telling us his name is showing us how close he is to us. His giving of the law on Sinai was another mark of his love for us; by observing it we agree to our part in his covenant of love. And as at this time we recall the names of those we love as we send them messages of greetings, so we recall that God remembers us in love. To the prophet Isaiah he said, "I have called you by your name, you are mine." And he has sent us Jesus Christ as a sign of love. In his name we are saved. St Peter says, "There is no other name under heaven given among men by which we must be saved." "Let your power take away our weakness," we pray, for he knows how to save us with outstretched arm and mighty power.

19 December

O Radix Jesse, qui stas in signo populorum, super quem continebunt reges os suum, quem gentes deprecabuntur: veni ad liberandum nos, jam noli tardare.

O Flower of Jesse's stem, you have been raised up as a sign for all peoples; kings stand silent in your presence; the nations bow down in worship before you. Come, let nothing keep you from coming to our aid. (ICEL)

O stock of Jesse, you stand as a signal for the nations; kings fall silent before you whom the peoples acclaim. O come to deliver us and do not delay. (Divine Office)

Isaiah 11:10 Romans 15:12 Isaiah 5:15 Habakkuk 2:3 Hebrews 10:37

Jesse, the father of King David, and an ancestor of Jesus Christ, founded a royal lineage. Jesus is the flower of Jesse's stem and stands as a banner for the nations. We are reminded of Jesus' words, "I, when I am lifted up from the earth, will draw all to myself." The words and actions of Christ are the rule against which governments and societies can be measured. The power of the Christian life to change the world must never be underestimated. Christians must respond to the plea for deliverance which has been heard in all ages, and is just as strong today throughout our world. And with great urgency it is made. And no situation is hopeless. It is when we feel that the bridegroom is long in coming that we must pray, "Come, Lord Jesus, do not delay; give new courage to your people who trust in your love."

20 December

O Clavis David, et sceptrum domus Israel: qui aperis, et nemo claudit; claudis, et nemo aperit: veni, et educ vinctum de domo carceris, sedentem in tenebris et umbra mortis.

O key of David, O royal Power of Israel controlling at your will the gate of heaven: come break down the prison walls of death for those who dwell in darkness and the shadow of death; and lead your captive people into freedom. (ICEL)

O key of David and sceptre of Israel, what you open no one else can close again; what you close no one can open. O come to lead the captive from prison; free those who sit in darkness and in the shadow of death. (Divine Office)

Isaiah 22:22 Revelation 3:7 Isaiah 42:6b-7 Psalm 107:14 Luke 1:79

"The king of life who died now lives and reigns." Christ has been raised from the dead; he is the first fruits of those who have fallen asleep. We rejoice that as by a man came death so by a man has come the resurrection of the dead. Christ has led us from captivity, brought us out of the prison. The key to the House of David, the kingdom of our God, has been given to him, and the good news of great joy is that he opens for us the gate to eternal life. Christmas celebrates birth and new life. We who live so often in the shadow of death can rejoice at this festival and give thanks to God who gives us the victory over the powers of death through Jesus Christ.

21 December

O Oriens, splendor lucis aeternae, et sol justitiae: veni, et illumina sedentes in tenebris et umbra mortis.

O Radiant Dawn, splendour of eternal light, sun of justice: come, shine on those who dwell in darkness and the shadow of death. (ICEL)

O Rising Sun, you are the splendour of eternal light and the sun of justice. O come and enlighten those who sit in darkness and in the shadow of death. (Divine Office)

Malachi 4:2 Hebrews 1:3 Luke 1:78-79 2 Peter 1:19 Isaiah 9:2

The festival of Christmas celebrates the Word made flesh, who came as a light in the darkness. The gospel of Christmas Day proclaims the true light who enlightens everyone. That light shines in our darkness and the darkness has not overcome it. There remain many days in winter from this shortest day until spring sunshine warms us once more. So also, in a world grown cold and dark through sin, we have to wait on God's grace. In our troubles and grief as we live in the shadow of death we have to let time heal. But through it all we keep our eyes open for the light of Christ, as St Peter exhorts us, "You do well to pay attention to this as to a lamp shining in a dark place, until the day dawns and the morning star rises in your hearts." And so we pray, "Let the light of the coming of your Son free us from the darkness of sin."

22 December

O Rex gentium, et desideratus earum, lapisque angularis, qui facis utraque unum: veni, et salva hominem, quem de limo formasti.

O King of all the nations, the only joy of every human heart; O Keystone of the mighty arch of man, come and save the creature you fashioned from the dust. (ICEL)

O king whom all the peoples desire, you are the cornerstone which makes all one. O come and save man whom you made from clay. (Divine Office).

Isaiah 28:16 Ephesians 2:14 Genesis 2:7

It is a king's task to build up a strong nation. Such a creation needs strong foundations. The story of God's people is a story of hopes and failures, of kings who put their trust in weak supports, who neglected to build on the strong support of the Lord God. The Christian, knowing that he is but dust of the earth, looks to Christ as the sure foundation. Kings and kingdoms, governments and nations come and go but Christ's kingdom shall never end. He is a king indeed, but his kingdom is not of this world. We are indeed earthen vessels, but we carry a treasure therein. For God has shone in our hearts giving the light of his knowledge in the face of Christ. He who led us out of darkness into his wonderful light has made us a chosen race, a royal priesthood, a holy nation.

23 December

O Emmanuel, Rex et legifer noster, expectatio gentium, et Salvator earum: veni ad salvandum nos Domine Deus noster.

O Emmanuel, king and lawgiver, desire of the nations, Saviour of all people, come and set us free, Lord our God. (ICEL)

O Immanuel, you are our king and judge, the one whom the peoples await and their Saviour. O come and save us, Lord, our God. (Divine Office).

Isaiah 7:14 Isaiah 8:8 Isaiah 33:22 Genesis 49:10

Our time of waiting is nearly over. We think of Mary in her waiting and expectation. She who bore a son whose name was Emmanuel — God with us — will lead us to Christmas peace and joy. We await a king and a law giver not in fear but in hope. The king will rule with justice and peace. He will make all things new. The law giver will make his law take root in our hearts, and there will be a new heart and a new spirit. And he is the one whom all people desire and await. In the expectations of young and old in the bustle of these days of preparation for Christmas there is seen that age old desire. All who wait in the darkness of suffering, of famine and drought, of homelessness and oppression and near despair, are longing for the one to come and save them. Our efforts to help make this world one of peace and hope will show indeed the Emmanuel — the God who is really with us all.

December 24

The initials of each antiphon in the Latin in inverse order create the acrostic ERO CRAS. The translation of this, "Tomorrow I shall be there", is seen as the answer of Christ to the prayers of the faithful during the past week.

```
        E
        R
        O
EROCRAS
        R
        A
        S
```

Isaiah in Advent

Wilfrid Harrington OP

Introduction

The Advent liturgy is not solely, nor even principally, a preparation for Christmas, the commemoration of the birth of Jesus. It is marked much more by expectation of the parousia, the second coming of Christ. And this is as it should be for we live in the age of his advent, the Messianic time. We cannot look forward to his first coming but, looking back to it, we can then turn our eyes to the time when the kingdom of God will be perfected. In this way we can still realistically share the expectation of Israel. It is not, then, surprising that Isaiah figures prominently in the readings, a prophetic book that is redolent with promise and hope.

A feature of the lectionary, and one without obvious significance, is that readings from Isaiah are almost wholly absent from Year C and occur in none of the Advent Sundays of that year. One might add that no Isaian passage occurs in the fourth week of Advent (apart from Is 7:10-14 [Dec 20] and 62:1-5 [Dec 24]). We shall be looking, then, at years A and B. It seems best to take the readings not haphazardly but in their Isaian sequence. In this way it is hoped more effectively to bring out their Advent message.

Isaiah

The first matter that needs to be taken care of is to outline the complex structure of the book of Isaiah and to note its broad chronological sweep. The acknowledged scholarly view is that Isaiah falls into three parts: Is 1-39 which contains oracles of the 8th-century prophet, Isaiah ben-Amoz; Is 40-55, known as Second Isaiah; and Is 56-66, often referred to as Third Isaiah. The background of Second Isaiah is the close of the Babylonian captivity, while Third Isaiah is set in Judah in the early days of the return. So far so good. But there is the complicating factor that, in Is 1-39, only chs 1-12 and 28-33 give, in the main, the words of Isaiah ben-Amoz.

We are not being pedantic. If one is to understand right a prophetical text it is enormously helpful to know its historical background. We cannot always be sure of a precise setting but it is helpful to know, at least, whether a text be early or late. In the present case I shall comment on the lectionary readings according to the threefold division of the book. This will involve setting certain passages from chs 1-39 in their appropriate chronological context. We shall see that the readings face up to different historical situations and we are thereby challenged to adapt those ancient messages to our historical situation and permit them to speak more directly to us.

I. The Words of Isaiah ben-Amoz
The vision of Isaiah the son of Amoz, which he saw concerning Judah and Jerusalem in the days of Uzziah, Jotham, Ahaz and Hezekiah, kings of Judah (1:1).

That title tells us nearly all we know of Isaiah. We can date his mission, in terms of the first and fourth kings listed, to between 783 and 687 B.C. His theological concern is manifestly that of Judah and Jerusalem. In Judah the promise to David, the Davidic covenant, (2 Sam 7) had replaced that of Sinai, and Zion with its temple was the new holy mountain. Hope for the future rested in the Davidic line: 'your house and your kingdom shall be made sure for ever before me; your throne shall be established for ever' (2 Sam 7:16). The king of Judah was 'son of God' (7:14). No enemy could destroy the holy city and the blessed dynasty. This conviction was the theological basis of Isaiah's hope in the face of seemingly inevitable disaster.

Judah had been prosperous under Uzziah and continued so under Jotham. Like Amos before him Isaiah attacked luxury and social abuses; this is the burden of many of the oracles of chs 1-5. The prophet's mission continued under Ahaz and to the end of the reign of Hezekiah. In 735, Ahaz, threatened by an anti-Assyrian coalition, appealed to the Assyrian king Tiglath-pileser and Judah became a vassal of Assyria. Isaiah insists on faith, the practical conviction that Yahweh alone matters. He vainly sought, in Ahaz, the faith which would turn the king from political alliances and enable him to stand, unperturbed, in the face of threats and even in the presence of hostile armies. Bluntly he warned him: 'If you will not believe, surely you will not be established' (7:9). Later, when Hezekiah, counting on Egyptian help, toyed with the notion of revolt, Isaiah opposed him too, and for the same reason. Yahweh, and he alone, will save the nation. For, despite the weakness and faithlessness of its kings, Zion, in the prophet's eyes, remained inviolable, because it was the dwelling-place of the holy God. Thus he could encourage Hezekiah when Sennacherib had over run Judah and had shut up the king 'like a bird in a cage'.

Is 2:1-5 (Year A First Sunday).

A passage from the earliest period of Isaiah's ministry. In the midst of denouncing sin, especially social sin, quite as vehemently as Amos, he endeavours to sustain hope. He paints an inspiring picture of what God has in store: justice between the nations, an end to wasteful war, the prosperity which will follow when people turn wholly to ways of peace. But peace can only be when all nations come to the mountain of the Lord; it cannot be accomplished without God. The meaning of Israel's election does not lie in the existence of the people as such but in the service which God demands. Israel must measure up to its task: to focus attention on the true God, the merciful God who desires the unity of the nations. There must be the creation of a new religious spirit when men and women will look to the true God 'that he may teach us his ways'. A challenge from that prophet of Judah to us Christians of today.

Is 7:10-14 (December 20).

Isaiah is vainly counselling his king, Ahaz, at a critical moment when the dynasty of David is in jeopardy (Is 7:1-6). The king's refusal to seek a sign comes not from piety (though he feigns piety) but from the fact that he had already made up his mind to reject the prophet's advice. Threatened by the allied forces of Syria and Israel he had determined to invite the intervention of the Assyrian super power; he has no confidence in the help of Yahweh. One does not so easily dispose of God: Ahaz will have his sign whether he wills or no. Isaiah had taken his stand on God's covenant with David (2 Sam 7). Each successive king of David's line personified the covenant relationship; each was a living reminder and guarantee of the covenant. Ahaz' queen is, at this moment of crisis, pregnant with the one who will continue the threatened line. Isaiah referred to the queen as a 'young woman'; the Greek translation runs: 'a virgin shall conceive'. Matthew (1:22-23) happily and rightly seized on it to bring out the fact that although every king of David's line did embody God's promise to be 'with us', only Jesus, son of the Virgin, did it perfectly.

Is 11:1-10 (Year A Second Sunday).

An oracle from a later period of Isaiah's ministry. He had been proved right in his assurance to Ahaz that Syria and Israel would not have their way. But the son of the 'young woman' (Hezekiah) had not measured up; he was no 'Immanuel'. The prophet's faith in the divine promise to David remained steadfast as ever but he looked now to a more distant future. He sketches his portrait of the true king. He will be a king spirit-endowed with the virtues of his ancestors: the wisdom and understanding of Solomon, the prudence and might of David, the knowledge and fear of the Lord of the patriarchs and prophets. Thus endowed he will rule with 'righteousness'. That is to say, he will champion the destitute and the oppressed. Furthermore, he will restore paradisal peace; the lovely image here has, justly, become proverbial. Prey and predator can feed and sleep in harmony; a child can keep an adder as a pet. All this is metaphor for that future in which distress will be no more and tears will be dried (Rev 7:15-17). It can only be when the earth will be full of 'the knowledge of the Lord'. That is, after all, our christian hope and our christian prayer: 'Thy kingdom come, thy will be done on earth . . .' We must let God be God in *his* way.

II. Second Isaiah

The author of Is 40-55, an anonymous prophet of the Exile, is, for convenience, named Second Isaiah. We have no inkling of the identity of this man, one of the foremost poets and theologians of Israel. All we do know is that he certainly belonged to the 'Isaian school' and found his inspiration in the work of his eighth-century predecessor. He foretells the end of the Babylonian exile and looks to the Holy One of Israel, the redeemer who will renew the miracles of the Exodus.

Is 40:1-11, 25-31 (Year B Second Sunday; Tuesday-Wednesday, Week 2)

The opening of the 'Book of Consolation'. The exuberant language of Second Isaiah serves a purpose. It is evident that there was little yearning for a return and the prophet has to drum up some enthusiasm. While, humanly speaking there were no grounds for optimism, he can assure his people that God is ready once again to bring them out of captivity to the promised land. This time Yahweh will lead them in solemn procession along a Via Sacra, a processional way hewn through mountain and valley and desert from Babylon to Jerusalem. This time there will be no years of wandering. God will manifest his glory (v.5) through his saving deed on behalf of his people. He is a constant God, unlike the ephemeral grass-like nature of humanity (vv 6-8). His 'word' stands for ever: 'For the mountains may depart and the hills be removed, but my steadfast love will not depart from you' (50:10). Jerusalem is bidden not only to welcome her God but to proclaim to the rest of Judah the good news of his coming. 'Good tidings' (v.9): it is here that the New Testament writers found their word 'Gospel', Good News.

The return from the Exile, begun in 537, fell far short of the glowing picture painted here. Later generations of Jews would have to await in patience the fulfilment of God's word. And the message of restoration might, too, be reinterpreted in moral terms: the highway to be made straight was the path of human life; the kingdom was to be prepared for by repentance. This text and a later understanding of it prepared for the fulfilment that came in the person of Jesus and was ushered in by the Baptist. In the New Testament (following the Greek version of Isaiah) he has become the 'voice crying in the wilderness' (Mk 1:3).

Is 40:25-31

The question is asked in v.18: 'To whom will you liken God?'; here we learn that he is the one who created the stars and 'names' them, i.e. rules them. The exiles are reminded (vv 27-31) that the creator God is also Lord of history; creator and redeemer, he acts with equal authority in nature and in history. He has not forgotten his exiled people and he is powerful to bring them back to their homeland — 'they who wait for the Lord shall renew their strength'.

Is 41:13-20 (Thursday, Week 2)

The passage 41:8-16 is the first of a series of oracles all giving a firm assurance of salvation (41:8-13, 14-16; 43:1-4, 5-7; 44:1-5). In the first and second of them, Yahweh acts directly so the pronoun 'I' recurs. God assures Israel not only that it will survive but that it will continue to be the object of his loving care. Israel may feel that it is nothing more than a 'worm' (v.14) but it enjoys the efficacious help of the Holy One of Israel (a favourite title of Yahweh throughout Second Isaiah). God is *go'el,* 'redeemer', the one who comes to the aid of a kinsman in trouble. In an image from primitive threshing procedure, Yahweh will use Israel as a solid threshing sled (with its iron teeth) to dispose of any who would hamper his design for his people. In vv 17-20 there is a return to the New Exodus theme. The exiles are the traditional poor and needy who stand in hopeful expectation before God. They hear the promise: 'I the God of Israel will not forsake them'. The Holy One of Israel creates this saving event: it is something he alone can do.

Is 45: 6-8, 18, 21-25 (Wednesday, Week 3)

Second Isaiah was convinced not alone that the meteoric rise of Cyrus had been guided by Yahweh but that Cyrus had been raised up for one purpose: 'he shall set my exiles free' (45:13). Where Assyria and Babylon had been rods of God's anger against his unfaithful people, Persia will be an instrument of their salvation. Clearly the prophet had an accurate perception of the character and policy of the emerging master of the world, but his presentation of a pagan ruler is unprecedented. Cyrus is the 'anointed', the Messiah, of the Lord (45:1) who declares of him: 'He is my shepherd, and he shall fulfil all my purpose' (44:28) and to him: 'I call you by your name, I surname you, though you do not know me' (45:4). Perhaps it would not be too fanciful to see in this approval of Cyrus an anticipation of Jesus' verdict on the exorcist who was not a disciple: 'he that is not against us is for us' (Mk 9:40).

The triumph of Cyrus and his benevolent deed on behalf of Israel will demonstrate the Godness of Yahweh (45:6-7). In Jerome's version, v8 had become an apt Advent prayer: 'Drop down dew ye heavens from above, and let the clouds rain the Just One'. Unhappily, like Joseph's technicolour coat, the original will not suffer that rendering. Those skies are bidden to rain down righteousness.

Verse 18 is a firm declaration that Yahweh's creative purpose was wholly positive. He had called a world out of chaos; his purpose is that it be a vibrant world of people. The logic of a God who is the only 'righteous God and Saviour' (v 21) emerges in v 22: 'Turn to me and be saved, all the ends of the earth'. For, if he stands alone as creator and redeemer, then humankind, for salvation, must look to him and to none other. There is the encouraging ring of universalism. Salvation is not for Israel only; it is for all who will accept salvation from the redeemer.

Is 48:17-19 (Friday, Week 3)

The main theme of ch 48 is that Yahweh had foretold the history of his people because he has never ceased to act in history. In the short passage vv 17-19 he carries three titles: Redeemer, Holy One of Israel, the Lord your God; his concern for Israel's welfare could hardly be more emphatically expressed. His desire is to lead them in 'the way you should go'. 'O that you had hearkened!' What is implied is the deuteronomic doctrine of the two ways: the way of life (of the commandments) or the way of death ('if your heart turns away' Dt 30:15-21). The same longing is poignantly expressed in Hos 11:2, 'the more I called them, the more they went from me'.

Is 54:1-10 (Thursday, Week 3)

This splendid hymn sings of Yahweh's enduring love. Hosea (chs 1-3) had set a trend: he had cast Yahweh as Husband of Israel. He was followed by his prophetic successors and by none more warmly than Second Isaiah in Ch 54. The barren spouse of Yahweh (the exile people) is called upon to sing for gladness: she will be made generously fruitful and must prepare for a multitude of children (vv 1-3). Again we meet an abundance of power-laden and promise-filled titles: Creator, Lord of hosts, God of the whole earth — but also Holy One of Israel and Redeemer. Israel may have been divorced but that divorce was temporary, not permanent (cf Hos 3). 'Great compassion' and 'everlasting love' quite outweigh 'wrath'. Here, in a nutshell, is the message of Second Isaiah (vv 4-8). Next, God's covenant with Noah is evoked (Gen 9:8-17): 'I establish my covenant with you . . . When the bow is in the clouds I will look upon it and remember the everlasting covenant'. Similarly, God's 'covenant of peace' with Israel will never be set at naught. Paul was thinking of the divine faithfulness when he declared of the Israel of his day: 'God has not rejected his people . . . for the gifts and the call of God are irrevocable' (Rom 11:2,29). 'Steadfast love *(hesed)* and 'covenant of peace' *(shalom)* signify abiding peace and wellbeing, gift of God's boundless compassion (vv 9-10). The promise looks to the future, the future of our christian prayer: 'Thy kingdom come, they will be done on earth'.

Is 29: 17-24 (Friday, Week 1)

A passage very like Second Isaiah. In terms of a marvellous transformation of nature, Lebanon, famous for its cedars, will become a luxuriant orchard. The author points to trans- formations in the human sphere. Deaf and blind will hear and see; the little ones and the poor will find joy. On the other hand, the ruthless will be brought low, the scoffer silenced and the perverters of justice confounded. By the remark that the meek and the poor 'exult in the Holy One of Israel' we are alerted to the fact that we have to do with the *anawim* who put their trust exclusively in the Lord. We have to do with a religious category. They are victims of the 'ruthless' and 'scoffer'. We are not too far removed in thought from the early chapters of the Book of Wisdom where the wicked are sworn enemies of the righteous (Wis 2-3). There are others than the wicked and the good; Is 29:22-24 looks to those who have erred but are open to salvation. The great things that God is about to do will stir them to conversion. We, who have witnessed the great thing God has done in sending his Son, should respond to that Son's call to *metanoia,* a change of heart.

Is 35:1-10 (Monday, Week 2)

Chapters 34 and 35 of Isaiah are closely related; they have been strongly influenced by Second Isaiah. Where ch 34 is a judgment on the nations (especially Edom, symbol of the enemies of God's people), ch 35 tells of Israel's future glory and blessedness, the one serving as a foil to the other. Modelling himself on Second Isaiah's description of return from the Exile, the new exodus (Is 40:3-5), the author of ch 35 envisages a wholesale return of Jews from the diaspora, a return to a transformed homeland (vv 3-4, 8-10). The messengers of this good news are bidden to have courage because their God is with them (vv 3-4). The notion of grace, in the broad sense of God's help to his people in need, is strong here. The image of the desert made fertile by rain from heaven (vv 6-7) holds out hope that a people, crushed by misfortune, will experience rebirth. Then, another image of hope, crippling disabilities such as blindness, deafness, lameness, will be relieved (vv 5-6). Mark had these verses in mind when he, at key points in his gospel, presented Jesus as healing a deaf man and a blind man (Mk 7:31-37; 8:22-26). For Christians, the thought of salvation should fill us with longing for deliverance from the inadequacies and imperfections of our present situation. In waiting, our courage tends to flag and we may fear that we might never achieve our rest. We are given hope and confidence by the presence of Christ in whom God's promise has become reality.

III. Third Isaiah

According to the generally accepted view, Is 56-66 is the work of a post-exilic prophet of the Isaian school and took shape in Palesine soon after the return from the Exile. The author addresses himself to the situation and conditions in the little province of Judah about 520 B.C., about the time of the prophets Haggai and Zechariah. There had been a return from the Exile but the situation was not all that the glowing promise of Second Isaiah might have led one to expect. City and temple are still in ruins; the economic state is deplorable; there is no organised community; some do not scruple to make a profit out of misery. But, in the midst of this situation the prophet voices the conviction that God's final intervention is at hand.

Is 56:1-8 (Friday, Week 3)

The post-exilic prophet makes known the will of Yahweh for his people, the true people of God, that they will open out to embrace even those who are not Israelite at all. In view of the nearness of God's deliverance the people are called upon to observe justice and righteousness. They achieve this not alone by keeping from evil but through religious observance (vv 1-2). According to Dt 23:1-3, eunuchs and certain foreigners might not enter the assembly of the Lord. Now such are to be made welcome. We meet in vv3-7 the universal sweep of Second Isaiah leading to the climactic declaration: 'my house shall be called a house of prayer for all peoples'. Evidently, the second temple is being built (it was dedicated in 515). That temple (no more than Herod's temple) never did welcome all nations. The statement is caught up by Mark in Jesus' words of judgment on the temple (Mk 11:17). In place of it he will build a temple 'not made with hands' (14:58), the temple of his community which will truly be open to all. In Is 56:8 the 'outcasts of Israel' are the returned exiles; Yahweh will bring others to swell their number.

Is 61:1-11 (Year B Sunday 3)

The prophet, speaking in the first person and catching up the words of the first Servant Song (Is 42:1), proclaims salvation. His 'anointing' by Yahweh is his missioning: to bring good tidings and proclaim liberation. His mission is to 'the poor', the *anawim,* those whose only resource is God. In the post-exilic situation such are also economically poor. He takes up and preaches again the message of salvation already urged by Second Isaiah (vv 1-3). He promises that Jerusalem will be restored. The Jewish people, as a priestly people, will be supported by the labour and wealth of the nations (vv 4-7); they will be renowned as a people blessed by the Lord (v 9).

The poem closes (vv 10-11) with the prophet, in the name of Zion, exulting with joy in the good news. Yahweh, whose activity is as sure as the cycle of nature, will clothe Zion in salvation and righteousness. The prophet's exuberance has the same purpose as that of Second Isaiah: in the midst of ruin and devastation, and resultant hopelessness, he holds out glowing promise. The Church, the new Jerusalem, should, so much more, be characterised by joyful hope. Hope is always the measure of faith. *Gaudium et spes*, joy and hope, fittingly describe the role of the Church and its message to our world. Any other message will not ring true.

Luke tells us that Jesus found in Is 61:1-2 the programme of his own ministry. Coming, one sabbath, to the synagogue of his native Nazareth, he opened the scroll of Isaiah and read out that passage. Then he declared: 'Today this scripture has been fulfilled in your hearing' (Lk 4:16-21). In this way a passage, notable in its own right, has been given startling relevance. Jesus made the prophecy his own. He is the Spirit-anointed one who preached good news to the poor. He manifested in his person the tender quality of the promised mercy.

Is 62:1-5 (December 24, Evening Mass)

The theme of salvation coming to Zion (ch 61) is continued in ch 62. The prophet will not cease to utter his message of hope and promise until Yahweh's saving deed shines forth and Zion's mourning is turned to joy. The glory of restored Zion, manifest to the nations, will be God's presence among his people. A new name will reflect a new status. She will be 'My-Delight-in-Her' and 'Married', no longer 'Forsaken' and 'Desolate'. The marriage image, noted in Second Isaiah, re-emerges. God, the saving and loving bridegroom, will rejoice over a bride whose beauty has been restored. One is reminded of Eph 5:25-27, 'Christ loved the Church and gave himself up for her . . . that the Church might be presented before him in splendour, without spot or wrinkle or any such thing, that she might be holy and without blemish.''

Is 63:16-17; 64:1-8 (Year B Sunday 1).

A reading taken from the long poem 63:7-64:12, a psalm of entreaty written while Jerusalem lay in ruins and the task of rebuilding the temple had not yet begun (of 64:10-11). It (and especially from 63:15 on) is typical of post-exilic prayers, the 'prayers of the chastened', in that it recalls God's goodness to his people and candidly acknowledges the people's ingratitude and sinfulness. The dominant note, however, is serene confidence in God's loving kindness. The opening statement, 'I will declare the steadfast love of the Lord' (v 7) does not just introduce a chronicle of his mercies of the past; it is assurance that his steadfast love reaches into the present. There is, too, an urgency about the psalm as it strives to bring its hearers to a recognition of their plight from which God alone can deliver them. Not only recognition but acknowledgment: they are expected to make this prayer their earnest prayer.

'Thou art our Father': the ancestors of Israel, the fathers Abraham and Jacob, lie silent and helpless in Sheol. But Israel is not fatherless. Yahweh is a living, present and acting father: father and redeemer of his people. Because God is one he is cause of everything, cause even of that hardening of heart that led to the disaster of the exile. This causality remained a mystery to the Israelite; it was never taken to diminish personal responsibility. Here the puzzled and pained question is put in the context of a confident prayer for God's gracious mercy (63:16-17). The prayer continues (64:1-5a) with a plea that God rend the veil of his heavenly abode and appear in a theophany more majestic than that of Sinai and bring deliverance to his people in distress. A confession of sin follows (vv 5b-7). His people had abandoned their God to their great loss. Jerusalem, the holy city of his dwelling, lies in ruins. Israel has become an unclean, polluted thing. It has cut itself off from the life giving source and has become a heap of withered leaves scattered to the winds. One is reminded that he is father, here creator of his people. Deliverance is readily within the power of the divine potter as he moulds, to his will, the clay of his people (vv 8-9).

Is 30:12-26 (Saturday, Week 1)
Written after the return from Babylon. There is the real-

isation that the historical restoration did not match the glowing picture of Second Isaiah: there has been ample cause for weeping. Soon, however, tears will be wiped away; the Lord will hear and answer. The Lord, source of wisdom, will be the one teacher; him alone they will come to heed. There is an echo here of Jer 31:31-34, no longer shall each man teach his neighbour and each his brother, saying, "Know the Lord", for they shall all know me'; the reason being that the law will be written upon their hearts. And we are reminded of the heavenly word at the transfiguration: 'This is my beloved Son, listen to him' (Mk 9:7), for he is our teacher. In Isaiah attention to the teacher will lead away from any pagan and idolatrous ways, a reference to abuses of the post-exilic period (Is 57:4-13;65:11-12;66:3-4). The joy of a resotration following on a change of heart is described in exuberant terms (30:23-26). Cf Is 60.

Is 25:6-10; 26:1-6 (Wednesday-Thursday, Week 1)

Chapters 24-27 of Isaiah are known as 'The Apocalypse of Isaiah'. In fact, they are not by Isaiah and are not truly apocalyptic. In thought, style and language the section is post-exilic but it is not possible to fix a precise date. What does seem assured is that Is 24-27 is the last product of that prolific Isaian school which had so long kept alive the spirit of the 8th century prophet.

Is 25:6-10

All nations are invited to a great eschatological banquet on Mt Zion. Tablefellowship means communion; it evokes friendship and peace. God will remove the veil of ignorance (covering) that had kept the nations from knowing him; the universalist thrust is manifest. There will be no more place for death and tears. The author of Revelation catches up the image of a tender parent comforting a weeping child: 'he will wipe away every tear from their eyes, and death shall be no more, neither shall there be mourning nor pain nor crying any more' (Rev 21:4). In the new Jerusalem sorrow and pain will have no place. Those who put their trust in Yahweh, those who have waited for him, will not be disappointed; they will rejoice in his salvation (Is 25:9; cf vv 6-8).

Is 26:1-6

Here the 'strong city' (v1) is contrasted with the 'lofty city' (v 5), God's city and the city of the proud. One is reminded of the Magnificat: 'he has put down the mighty from their thrones, and exalted those of low degree' (Lk 1:52). God himself is the fortification of his city, the everlasting rock. The poet is thinking of a rebuilt Jerusalem; the 'righteous people' are the returned exiles. It would be difficult to find a better expression than v 3 of the tranquillity of heart that comes with total trust in a gracious God; 'Thou dost keep him in perfect peace, whose mind is stayed on thee, because he trusts in thee.' This is the peace that Jesus offers: 'Peace I leave you; my peace I give to you. Let not your hearts be troubled, neither let them be afraid' (Jn 14:27). Peace: surely an Advent sentiment, an Advent blessing.

Reflection

We have seen that the Advent readings come from all three sections of Isaiah. As such, they reflect three historical situations in the experience of Israel. Their common theme is a looking to a promise filled future. There is a pervading note of hope firmly sustained by trust in a faithful and forgiving God. Our life as a Christian people may be more similar than we care to acknowledge to that of the Israel of Isaiah.

1. Isaiah ben-Amoz stands as a prophet of faith, there is no doubt of that. All the more does he hold a salutary lesson for us. A century after him, when Judah was threatened by Babylon, successor to Assyria, Jeremiah faced an impossible task in striving to convince his contemporaries that Nebuchadnezzar, unlike Sennacherib, would have his way and that Zion and its temple would perish. He was not believed. What Yahweh had done in the days of Hezekiah he would

surely do and continue to do. The son of David was son of Yahweh; Zion was city of Yahweh; the temple was his dwelling-place. A young Jeremiah would have adhered to the given theology, the comforting theology of a promissory covenant. An older Jeremiah, faced with the patent failure of the Davidic monarchy, looked back to a covenant. What he was sure of, in the teeth of disaster, was that Yahweh could and would pick up the pieces and put them together again. Yahweh could do what 'all the king's horses and all the king's men' could not do. Second Isaiah would be heir to Jeremiah.

For Isaiah, the traditional theology could still work, could still make sense. For Jeremiah, not in a very different situation (the Assyrian threat had been painfully real), it no longer made sense. He had to look for another theology, one that really faced up to his situation. Isaiah had looked for an Immanuel, the ideal Davidic king. He would never have recognised that future king in a helpless victim on a cross. One feels that Jeremiah might find him there. And Second Isaiah, with his Songs of the Suffering Servant, surely would. Isaiah (that eight century prophet) when put in perspective, alerts one to the fragility of any tidy theological system. God will not be confined. He must be allowed to surprise us. While our faith should grow in firmness, our theology should ever be open, open to the breath of the Spirit, alert to the 'signs of the time'.

II. Deuteronomy proposes a doctrine of the 'two ways': the way of faithfulness to God and his commandments, the way of life; the way of infidelity, the way of death (Dt 30:15-20). In Judges this deuteronomic doctrine is illustrated in terms of a recurring cycle: infidelity – disaster – repentance – deliverance (Jg 2:6-3:6). The deuteronomists offered an explanation of the unparalleled disaster that was the destruction of Jerusalem and the Exile. The bottom had fallen out of Judah's world. Yahweh's promises to the patriarchs and to David had gone up in smoke. Was Yahweh a God incapable of protecting and sustaining his people? No; the key to the disaster was the fatal choice of the people: they had walked the way of death. It is not too late. They may still choose life; they may still get back on the right way. Repentance, *metanoia,* will, without fail, lead to deliverance and restoration.

Second Isaiah assumes that those he addresses had learned the deuteronomic lesson. They have come to their senses and have turned back to their God. They are poised for deliverance. He bends his evident poetic talent to the expression of his fervent conviction. There will be, unquestionably, a new Exodus. There will be a fresh flowering. The aftermath would show that the reality did not measure up to his expectation. But there was a change, irreversible. There was a return and a new phase of life for Judah. The enthusiasm he had drummed up was not sustained but he had started something, he had awakened his people to a new understanding of themselves and of their God. His universalist vision was an inspiration and a challenge.

The history of life in Judah in the centuries after the return was to show that, sadly, his vision was lost to sight. The community had found its way but, more and more, that way became *its* way. No longer was there gross infidelity. Instead, fidelity became an obsession. Faithfulness lay in meticulous observance of commandments, statutes and ritual. It follows that God could no longer be, truly, a universal God. He could only be the God of those who served him according to the minutiae of Torah.

We are reminded of Vatican II and the post-conciliar Church. The Council, in the celebrated image of John XXIII, was an opening of windows, a letting the wind of the Spirit blow through. It was an opening of minds. There can be no going back. But there has been a hardening — there is no doubt of that. There is a certain yearning for a more secure but more closed Church. We Christians might remind ourselves that we are expected to mediate the invitation of our

God, 'Turn to me and be saved, all the ends of the earth'
(Is 45:22).

III. What does one do when reality does not match up to expectation? One can throw in the towel and bow to the
'inevitable'. But someone has said: 'Better to light a candle
than curse the dark'. In the despondancy of post-exilic gloom
Third Isaiah dared to hold aloft the torch of his starry
eyed predecessor. True, Second Isaiah seemed to be a romantic visionary. But he could and did cry out: 'I have a dream!'
The dream of Martin Luther King has not wholly taken shape.
But would his people have reached where they are now
without his dream? John XXIII, we had fondly thought, had
exorcised the 'prophets of doom'. They are a sturdy breed
and are still with us. Third Isaiah, like Second Isaiah, reminds
us Christians of hope. It has always seemed to me that a pessi-
mistic Christian is a contradiction in terms. Do we, or do we
not, believe in the promise of our God? The wild exuberance
of those prophets echoes the extravagance of their God. 'Only
God's wild laughter / could hope that things will turn out
even' (Brendan Kennelly).

We, in Advent, look to victory. That victory was inaugurat-
ed in a humble birth. Salvation, the salvation of humans, has
to be a salvation within human life. Inevitably, our salvation,
begun with birth, ended in death. There is little sense in
acknowledging a 'gentle Jesus, meek and mild' unless we are
prepared to admit that that graceful baby would grow up to
be one despised and rejected and nailed to a cross. What we
need to admit, simply and directly, is the shocking truth that
our saviour is present, wholly, completely, in the little babe,
in the adolescent, in the workman, in the preacher, in the
condemned criminal. Mark and Paul are wholly right. One
cannot see God in the face of Christ Jesus if one is not prepared to face the shattering truth of the cross.

The widespreading 'Isaiah' can be a help to us. There is
Immanuel, God-with-us, who might seem to be some Jack-in-
the-box: all one needs is trust in David and Zion and, hey

presto, all is well. There is that irrepressible optimist, Second Isaiah, who believes wholly in his dream and who carried others with him. And that other, Third Isaiah, faced with the toughest task of all. Second Isaiah had sparked a return. It fell to his successor to cope with bitter disillusionment. How does one bring hope to people in a trough of despair? One surely does not do it by underlining their misery. One paints a vision and confidently proclaims the impossible. There is Resurrection beyond the Cross. And all because there is God. We look for the advent not only of the life of birth and of the life beyond death. We look to the God 'who gives life to the dead and calls into existence the things that do not exist' (Rom 4:17).

Mary and Advent

Christopher O'Donnell, O Carm

The origins of the Advent season are complex, coming from the traditions of East and West, centering on both the Epiphany and the feast of Christmas and taking a penitential character from the Roman Ember Days as well as from the parallel with Lent. The *General Norms for the Liturgical Year* found in the beginning of the Roman Missal summarise the meaning of the whole season:

> The season of Advent has a twofold character. It is a time of preparation for Christmas when the first coming of God's Son to men is recalled. It is also a season when minds are directed by this memorial to Christ's second coming at the end of time. It is thus a season of joyful and spiritual expectation (n.39).

As we now celebrate it, Advent is in two parts each with its dominant characteristic. Up to 16 December the main note is eschatological: there is a strong emphasis on penance and on being ready when Christ comes in glory. From 17 December the mood changes and the season becomes largely a preparation for Christmas. In the first part of the season the main figure is John the Baptist. He proclaimed the coming of the kingdom whose final manifestation we still await. Mary is the dominant personage of the second part of the season though she is not entirely absent from the earlier part, most notably in the Midday Prayer of the Liturgy of the Hours which continually recalls the Annunciation and celebrates her virginity.

This article first appeared in *Scripture in Church,* issue 36, Dominican Publications, St. Saviour's, Dublin 1 and is reproduced by permission.

The Advent Virgin

The key-note of Advent is expectancy: it is the future tense that predominates in antiphons, prayers and readings, just as it does in the infancy gospels of Matthew and Luke. This mood of expectancy occurs strongly in the assertion that 'we watch for the day, hoping that the salvation promised us will be ours when Christ our Lord will come again in his glory' (Advent Preface 1).

From 17 December we are called upon to await the coming of Christ 'our hearts filled with wonder and praise' (advent Preface II).

In his exhortation, *Marialis cultus* (1974), Pope Paul VI invites us to take Mary as model for our Advent spirituality. We do this not only by looking to the very many references to her in the liturgy, but by seeking to adopt her attitude.

> . . . living in the spirit of Advent, by thinking of the inexpressible love with which the Virgin Mother awaited her Son, we are invited to take her as a model and to prepare to meet the Saviour who is to come (n.4).

In each liturgical season we are to be formed by the word of God which the Church presents to us. Mary is our model in being listeners of the word. Clearly she was always dedicated to the scriptures. But we can only surmise the joy with which she would have gone to the synagogue in the nine months after the Annunciation to hear the Law and the Prophets read. We can try to enter into what must have been her mind as she heard the ancient texts and prayers which expressed the longings of her people for God's Holy One. How eager she must have been to learn what might be said about her son. Mary's Sabbath attitude, her thirst for the word of God would have continued throughout her life. Indeed, she would have taught her son Jesus the traditions of his people, and later learned from him the fulness of the mystery of God, hidden for ages and now being worked out through both their lives. This image of Mary as the Sabbath Virgin is one to guide us in the days of Advent: we too must

91

hear the word of God with eagerness to learn God's plan, to know her son.

But it is not enough to hear God's word, even with expectancy. We must like Mary ponder it in our hearts (cf Lk 2:19, 51). The Greek expression of Luke evokes the idea of 'throwing together' various elements in order to find their inner meaning, somewhat like the wise man in Sirach 39:1-3. Mary is confronted by God's message through revelation (Annunciation and the shepherds), through events, through the scriptures. She does not understand all at once (cf Lk 1:29,34;2: 48,50). She must keep reflecting on the word of God (and this in the rich Hebrew sense of 'word' being what is said and done by God). Mary is thus the perfect examplar of the good ground on which the seed of the word of God is sown (cf Lk 8:11):

> The seed on good ground are those who hear the word in a spirit of openness, retain it, and bear fruit through perseverence (8:15).

Mary heard the word of God, she pondered it in her heart. But she is to be numbered among those who are blest because they not only hear the word of God but keep it and put it into practice (cf Lk 11:28). The Advent Virgin is a woman of faith. Her faith is profoundly seen in her total 'yes' at the Annunciation (Gospel, 20 December). She declares herself to be the slave of the Lord (cf Lk 1:38 where 'servant' or 'handmaid' are both too weak as translations of *doulē).* A slave is one with few or no rights. Mary stands before God so that his will be fully done in her.

We find the theme of Mary, woman of faith, very strongly in the gospel of the Fourth Sunday of this year's liturgy. There is a significant parallel between the praise of Mary by Elizabeth and the incident of the woman in the crowd in Luke:

Blessed are you among women and blessed is the fruit of your womb . . . Blessed is she who believed	Blessed is the womb that bore you and the breasts that you sucked . . . Blessed rather are those

that there would be a fulfilment of what was spoken to her from the Lord. (Lk 1:42-45).

who hear the word of God and keep it. (Lk 11:27-28).

In both we begin with praise for Mary's physical maternity: she is blessed as Mother of Jesus (cf. 'she bore him in her womb with love beyond all telling' *Advent Preface II).* But there is an immediate progression to her faith: she is blessed because she believed, she heard the word of God and kept it.

It is in the light of this picture of Mary in her Sabbath disposition, pondering the word of God, being the woman of faith that we can approach the liturgical texts of Advent. She is our model as we enter into the mystery of the Incarnation, a mystery of the Father's love in Son and Mother.

In the days beginning 17 December we have the readings of major messianic texts from the Old Testament. In our context we can see in the blessed women of the Old Testament clear figures of Mary, Mother of the Messiah. In her, as in them, it is by the mighty act of God alone that his plans are fulfilled. The power of God makes the barrenness of the women of promise fruitful, e.g. mother of Samson (19 December, Jdg 13), Hannah (22 December, 1 Sam 1), Elizabeth (19 December, Lk 1). In a much more elevated way Mary's virginity is transformed through the overshadowing of the Holy Spirit so that she remains Ever Virgin and Mother of the Saviour. The liturgy recalls this power of God to transform in such prayers as:

'Let your power take away our weakness' (19 December, Mass);

'You will bring us good news and power that will transform our lives'. (17 December, Evening Prayer).

Mary is the perfect exemplar of God's power manifest in weakness. Looking at the lowliness of his servant, he does great things for her (cf. Lk 1:48-49).

The main motifs of Luke's infancy gospel are all recalled in the readings and prayers of these pre-Christmas days. Each allows us to penetrate still a little into the mystery of Mary. Central to the infancy narrative are the *anawim,* the poor of the Lord who have learned to place their hope in him alone (cf. Zeph 3:14). Elizabeth and Zechariah, the shepherds and later Simeon and Anna are all *anawim* figures. But the Second Vatican Council notes that Mary . . .

> stands out among the poor and humble of the Lord who confidently hope for and receive salvation from him (*Church* n. 55).

The poverty of Mary is most profoundly seen in her trust in the Lord, in her recognition that she is rich in him (cf Lk 1:49-53). Our Advent preparation is a recognition of our weakness so that God's power may triumph in our lives (cf 2 Cor 12:7-10).

The infancy gospels and the Advent liturgy constantly remind us of the Holy Spirit and the power of God (cf Lk 1:15,35,41; also 2:25-27):

> Give us your Spirit so that we may be radiant with his light (17 December, Mass).
> God of love and mercy, help us to follow the example of Mary always ready to do your will. At the message of an angel she welcomed your eternal Son and, filled with the light of your Spirit, she became the temple of your Word (20 December Mass).
> The Son of Man is coming with great power (17 December, Evening Prayer).

Another major theme is that of rejoicing (cf Lk 1:14,28,44, 47). We may say with the Litany of Loreto that Mary is 'Cause of our Joy' because she is 'Ark of the Covenant'. Just as God's power hovered over the ark in the Old Testament (cf Ex 40:35), so the Holy Spirit overshadowed Mary (cf Lk 1:35). The ark was the privileged place of God's presence to his people. Mary, who visits Elizabeth, brings a new presence of God to her, so that she and the unborn John the Baptist are blessed. Through Mary we have Emmanuel, God-with-us (cf 4th Sunday Mass, Year C).

Immaculate Conception

The date of the Immaculate Conception was established through the earlier feast of the Nativity of Mary, a feast of Jerusalem origin celebrated nine months earlier. Though it belongs, therefore, more properly to the sanctoral cycle of celebrations rather that to the seasonal cycle, we can, none-theless, see it as a jewel of the Advent liturgy. In *Marialis cultus* Pope Paul noted that 8 December is:

> a joint celebration of the Immaculate Conception of Mary, of basic preparation (cf Is 11:1-10) for the coming of the Saviour and of the happy beginning of the Church without spot or wrinkle (n. 3).

Modern mariology looks at the dogmas about Mary from a double focus: it sees in them Mary's relationship to the Church and her relationship to her Son. In this way the Immaculate Conception is clearly the preparation of Mary to be Mother of God. But by this gift she is also model of all the Church seeks to be. These two ideas are found in the Preface of the feast which interweaves both aspects of the mystery:

> You allowed no stain of Adam's sin to touch the Virgin Mary. Full of grace, she was to be a worthy mother of your Son, your sign of favour to the Church at its begin-ning, and the promise of its perfection as the bride of Christ, radiant in beauty. Purest of virgins, she was to bring forth your Son, the innocent lamb who takes away our sins. You chose her from all women to be our advocate with you and our pattern of holiness.

There are other rich ideas also to be found in the liturgy of that day: God's choice and election (readings at Midday Prayer), the blessedness of Mary (antiphons throughout Liturgy of Hours and notably in the second reading from St Anselm), our need to be preserved sinless (all prayers of Mass). Mary's Immaculate Conception does not remove her from us. Rather as we celebrate God's mercy towards her, we are strengthened in our personal hope to receive that same mercy which will also keep us free from sin.

Conclusion

It is in its *Constitution on the Liturgy* rather than elsewhere that we find what is perhaps the most profound statement of the Second Vatican Council about Mary. We can place in an Advent context the key ideas of this document:

> In celebrating this annual cycle of *the mysteries of Christ* Holy Church honours the Blessed Virgin Mary, Mother of God, with a *special love.*
>
> *She is inseparably linked* with her Son's saving work.
>
> In her the Church admires and exalts *the most excellent fruit of redemption,*
>
> and joyfully contemplates, as in a *faultless image,* that which she herself desires and hopes wholly to be (n. 103).

As we honour the Advent Virgin it is in the celebration of the *mysteries of Christ.* There is no authentic devotion to Mary that is not more profoundly worship of her Son and ordered to his glory. Advent which brings us into the heart of the mystery of the Incarnation is also a time when we honour her with *special love.* The Office of Readings for 20 December has an extract from the well known homily of St Bernard who pictures the whole world awaiting the reply of Mary to the angel:

> Answer, O Virgin, answer the angel speedily; rather through the angel, answer your Lord. Speak the word, and receive the Word; offer what is yours, and conceive what is of God; give what is temporal, and embrace what is eternal.

The special love of the Church at this time is in gratitude to her who consented to become the Mother of the Lord, and who walked in faith to the foot of the cross.

From the beginning she is *inseparably linked* with her Son's saving work. This union of Mother and Son began at the Annunciation. But the Advent liturgy brings us deeper into the mystery of a redemptive incarnation. We do indeed rejoice at the coming of the Saviour through Mary, but we know that in this "he humbled himself to come among us as a man, he fulfilled the plan you formed long ago and opened for us the way to salvation' (Advent Preface I). And this path of humiliation would lead to the desolation of the cross.

Mary is admired and exalted as the *most excellent fruit of redemption.* Her Immaculate Conception is already the saving work of Jesus operative for his mother to keep her free from sin. This preservation means that Mary is truly redeemed. And so we can see her as a *faultless image* of all the Church desires and hopes wholly to be. The Advent season in preparing for the two comings of Jesus brings together the two mysteries of the Immaculate Conception and the Assumption. In her sinlessness she is the image of what the Church desires to be. We seek to be ever more free from evil and guilt. But in Advent we are also saying 'come' as we await in hope the appearance of the Lord in glory. But what we look forward to and prepare ourselves for is already fulfilled in Mary's Assumption. She has fully entered into glory. We, therefore, celebrate in Advent what Mary has already achieved.

The liturgy of this season confers on the Church a twofold blesssing. It invites the Church to take Mary as its model, the woman of faith. With her dispositions we are to prepare for the coming of the Lord. At the same time it draws us into deeper contemplation of the wonders of God's power at work in her, so that we can praise him for it as we learn more profoundly the meaning of the *Magnificat:* 'he who is mighty has done great things for me'. This can be seen as summarised in the feast which follows the Advent liturgy, the Solemnity of Mary, Mother of God:

Father, source of light in every age,
the Virgin conceived and bore your Son
who is called Wonderful God, Prince of Peace.
May her prayer, the gift of a mother's love,
be your people's joy through all ages.
May her response, born of a humble heart,
draw your Spirit to rest on your people (Prayer of Mass).

The Liturgy of the Hours in Advent

Sean Collins OFM

The nature of the Liturgy of the Hours as the praise of God and the assimilation of his saving work in and through the symbol of time has not, in spite of the change in designation in the 1971 revision of the Breviary, been generally perceived at the practical level. The Hours are still thought of as simply Scripture services, or as a prepackaged quantity of 'divine praise' which certain members of the Church take upon themselves to offer to God.

In a fine little book on celebrating Evening Prayer in the parish setting, Laurence Mayer makes the point that 'no authority can take credit for discovering morning and evening . . . a people gathers in prayer, not in response to the *idea* of a sunset, but to the *event,* to-day's end and night's coming'[1]. The same author holds that the Hours as an experience of passing time, especially in its most visible moments of transition of day to night and night to new day, must always be their main focus as prayer, and that this focus should never be lost sight of in accomodating liturgical seasons. Since the central mystery of the Advent season, however, is precisely the experience of time — past, present and future — as filled with the promise of God, Hours and season combine and reinforce one another in an exceptionally powerful way and together offer us a unified symbolic framework.

It might even be said that in Advent the Hours carry the core experience of the season even more vividly than the Eucharistic celebrations. The Eucharist celebrates presence and relationships forged in the sharing of the bread and the cup — though of course it also stresses the proleptic and anticipatory nature of the experience of the Kingdom which it contains. The Hours, which make of the very flux of time itself the filter through which salvation is experienced, speak to our ambiguities, our hopes and our fears. In them the impassioned plea, 'O that you would tear asunder the heavens and come down!' (Is 64:1), resounds in all its urgency and existential force; the cry, 'Watchman, what of the night?' (Is 21:11), carries within itself both the threat of encroaching chaos and an anguished yearning for meaning and reassurance. In the Advent Liturgy of the Hours a pattern is given us within which we can both confront the terror of contingency and human powerlessness and, because its symbolism enables us to cope with what is otherwise a numbing and unthematised dread, renew our hope in the God who is Lord of the future.[2]

Time, Alienation and Advent
It is more than a little incongruous to hear Christians lamenting the 'hijacking' of Christmas by 'pagan consumerism and revelry'. The fact is, of course, that Christians themselves hijacked the festival for their own purposes many centuries ago. Those who put Christ into the Saturnalia can scarcely complain that so many nowadays are leaving him out again! The celebration of the winter solstice is the outward manifestation of the massive sigh of relief of the collective psyche when the corner is turned and the relentless onset of cold and darkness is checked. Cold and darkness are archetypal symbols: none of us is indifferent to them at gut level. They represent everything we fear, all the unknown forces which can isolate and crush us. The flaring fire, the orgy of feasting in the midst of winter is an affirmation of life. It says: 'Look! Nature is benign after all. We are justified in being optimistic. The final outcome of things will favour us.'

Our ancestors who built the neolithic structures of the Boyne Valley expressed in their celebration of the solstice 'the happiness of belonging to the ultimately kind cosmic ground, the source of peace beyond the struggle between life and death'.[3] That Christians should attribute their confidence about such kindness and peace to Christ is not surprising, and that they would press the symbolism of the solstice into service is understandable. But the risk is there that when Christ no longer means the assurance of ultimate well-being to people, and they are deprived of any other satisfactory mythical and symbolic reference pattern their fears will not adequately be uncovered and their need of reassurance will be expressed in frenetic snatching at illusory festivity.

Advent is the Christian expression of both fear and reassurance; it serves an invaluable function in equipping believers to cope with the future. It is essential that it first enables us to name what threatens us, since without that there is no escaping it. When this is not done Advent inevitably becomes a pious play-acting unworthy of adult people, a make-believe 'preparation' for the coming of a cuddly Baby Jesus whose only function is to pander to our regressive tendencies. The Advent Liturgy of the Hours takes its symbolism largely from Isaiah, a collection of prophecies launched into the teeth of chaos, political and social. This is not fortuitous. The purpose of the exercise is not to acquaint us with the various Isaiahs so much as to use the splendid imagery and haunting poetry of the book as a means to uncover and reveal to us the situations in which we need to open ourselves to the presence and promise of God.

The lyrical quality of the office in Advent

Variable antiphons are the principal means relied upon by the Latin Office to reflect the atmosphere of a feast or season. Most of the reformation Churches rejected even this device as an irrelevant interruption of the continuous perusal of the Psalter — with the result that in reformed Common Prayer it was difficult to divine whether one was celebrating Christmas Day or Good Friday until one arrived at the concluding prayer.

This stands in marked contrast to the Eastern Offices, which allow the Church's own lyrical reflection on feasts and seasons (in the shape of troparia which have over the centuries been combined into various forms in the different hours of the day and night) to predominate to the extent that the poetic texts often displace the Scriptural texts upon which they were initially a commentary.

Advent, which has no exact parallel in the Eastern Churches, is the season in which the lyrical component of the Latin Office is at its most intense. The antiphons and responsories are predominantly borrowed from Isaiah's vision of messianic fulfillment. This differs from the usual practice of taking the antiphon from the Psalm which it accompanies, and it ensures that the seasonal theme is a kind of counterpoint regularly recurring throughout the Offices. The result is an inner tension which often contrasts the radiant vision of the antiphons with the reality of everyday struggle and disillusionment regularly mirrored in the psalms. But such a juxtaposition is exactly what we experience in trying to live as Christians in a secular society. The daily search for meaning and pattern in the disjointed happenstances of life can at best come up with glimpses of the *Erchomenos* — the One who Comes, new every morning, as the future in our midst. The conviction that life is 'all glorious within',[4] in spite of the ambiguities which beset us, is one which must be continually reinforced, but it is of inestimable value in living coherently and creatively. The Advent Hours provide an experience of the fragility of vision and of its nevertheless compelling power, and thus offer a symbolic structure to our hopes and fears and a resolution in joyous expectancy to the ambiguity of time.

The power of these lyrical texts of the Office (which are 'poetic' in the sense of creative) is perfectly exemplified in the famous *'Aspiciens a longe'* Responsory of Readings on the First Sunday of Advent.[5]

This usually long Responsory is a catena of Psalm verses in which the watchman, gazing from his high tower, describes in the distance a stranger approaching from out of the dark night. He exhorts the hearers to go out and ask the stranger 'Are you he who is to come?' The one coming is addressed as

'Shepherd of Israel' and 'King of glory' — but his identity is still not clear. And the repetition of question and acclamation arouses all the echoes of our Advent waiting. The 'cloud covering all the earth', which makes recognition of the stranger difficult, is a potent symbol of everything that is alienating and destructive. It would not be too fanciful to see in it the ultimate threat, the ominous mushroom cloud which is the menacing backdrop to all our contemporary experience of time.

Because of the power of its symbolism, the Advent liturgy is effective. It engages the emotional response of people of all times and backgrounds. Even though the splendid chant 'Rorate, caeli, desuper' is not officially part of the Advent Liturgy of the Hours, it exemplifies how Isaian texts can be woven together[6] in such a way as to involve the hearer in the poignant vision of desolation and ruin and in the hope that the 'Holy One of Israel, your Redeemer' is coming to save.

Advent Hymnody

The selection of Advent hymns in the *Divine Office* is meagre (though it reflects the Latin *Liturgia Horarum* which has only one set of hymns for each of the two parts of Advent). The rich hymnody developed by the Protestant Churches was often a substitute for the drastic elimination by the reformers of antiphons and responsories, and is capable of conveying the flavour of a season in a pleasant way. The *General Instruction on the Liturgy of the Hours* points out that hymns 'constitute a popular part of the Hours, since they nearly always point more immediately than the other parts of the Office to the individual characteristics of the Hours or of each feast. They help to move the people taking part and draw them into the celebration. Their literary beauty often increases their effectiveness. In the Office, the hymns are the principal poetic part composed by the Church' (GILH 173).

Hymns should, therefore, be chosen carefully to enhance the celebration of the Hours. The freedom to use a wider choice of hymns, provided they are suited to their purpose, offered in GILH 178, should be availed of. They should not be metrical versions of Scriptures, for instance psalms, but an explicitly Christian reflection on the mystery being celebrated. In Advent this mystery is linked with the coming of the Lord and his offer of salvation amid 'the changes and chances of this fleeting life'. St Bernard of Clairvaux, following tradition, speaks in the second lesson of Wednesday of Week 1 of Advent of a threefold coming of the Lord: the first when the Lord was seen on earth and lived among men, the second, when he will be seen by all mankind as he comes in glory, and the third, which takes place between the other two and whose chief characteristic, according to Bernard, is that it is not seen. This is the invisible coming of Christ amid the ambiguity of passing time, the arena of salvation and the chief object of the celebration of the Liturgy of the Hours. Philip Doddridge's well-known hymn *Hark the glad sound! The Saviour comes!*[7] is an excellent example of a celebration of the 'silent coming between the other two':

> Hark the glad sound! The Saviour comes,
> The Saviour promised long:
> Let every heart prepare a throne
> And every voice a song.

The *hetoimasia,* or prepared throne, is a feature of the apse mosaics of early Christian churches; it was waiting in readiness for Christ, the Lord. Preparing a throne in our hearts means living in readiness, discerning the silent signs of Christ's coming and welcoming him as Lord. The hymn, in Doddridge's original manuscript, is headed: Christ's message from Luke 4:18,19. The liberation there proclaimed by Jesus is reflected in the other verses of the hymn: Christ comes to release prisoners, to bind broken hearts, to bring wealth to the poor. The implication is that we, who hymn Christ's coming with 'glad Hosannas', must be aligned with him for whom we have prepared a throne in his work of liberation, and in fact *be* his advent into situations of deprivation and unfreedom today.

Doddridge's hymn might not be suitable, in its dated

language and rigid metre, to a modern congregation (mercifully, a rather weird verse which announces that Christ comes 'on the eyeballs of the blind to pour celestial day' is omitted in most hymnals!). But its concerns and its urgency are a headline to those who are concerned to celebrate the season in a way that is in keeping with the nature of the Office and relevant to people's lives.

The Office of Readings

It is clear from GILH 55 that the Office of Readings is not really a liturgy of time, but rather 'a more extensive meditation on sacred scripture and on the best writings of spiritual authors' intended particularly for 'those who are consecrated to God in a special way'. Nevertheless, when it is celebrated at night it becomes a symbol of the Church's watch for the coming of the bridegroom — a theme especially congenial to Advent, and which is captured in Philip Nicolai's *Wachet auf* ('Wake, O wake, for night is flying').

All the scripture readings for Advent are taken from Isaiah. The original project for the Office of Readings had a two-year cycle, of which the present set was year two. Year one included, as well as sections from Isaiah, passages from the Books of Ruth, 1 Chronicles and Micah. But the two-year cycle has not been implemented.

The collection of texts under the name of Isaiah are used in most traditions in Advent. They reflect a turbulent political and social scene over a long period of time. And yet they breathe, in majestic language, a sense of hope and of an assured future. Chaos is resolved, adverse circumstances become God's instruments, human fickleness and malice fail to impede the triumphant progress of a chosen people. The vivid images of Advent — the blasted stump of Jesse which unexpectedly sprouts again, the desert becoming a carpet of blossom, darkest night giving way to brilliant noonday — these are the stuff of symbolism, and they enable us to cope with nuclear threat and personal spiritual bankruptcy, since reality is of a piece and the miracles of God's care are ever renewed. 'Remember not the former things, nor consider the things of old. Behold, I am doing a new thing; now it springs forth, do you not perceive it? I will make a way in the wilderness and rivers in the desert' (Is 43:18-19).

The selection of readings from the Fathers in the second lesson is somewhat narrow. The most recent writer (apart from some texts of the Second Vatican Council) is Saint John of the Cross — and he died in 1591. No women are represented. The readings for the last days of Advent (December 17-24) are well chosen commentaries on the gospels for those days, but one would wish to add to the selection for the first part of the season. Books like Maria Boulding's *The Coming of God*[8] are imbued with the scriptures and are yet contemporary in their style and content. The Advent pieces in Ronald Knox's *Stimuli*[9] might have been written as lessons for the Office, as to length — and they are in English, as opposed to being translations from Latin and Greek which often obscure the clarity of an Augustine or a Chrysostom. Many similar examples could be found which could point our Advent reflection and direct it towards our world.

Winter nights lead themselves to quiet reflection and prayer. In the winter darkness people gather together in the firelight and tell stories; the environment is hostile outside, and there is comfort in company. In the summertime nature is our playground and we feel fully at home in the world; the solidarity of our fireside gatherings is not necessary. Summer is the time of fulfillment, winter of remembering and longing. To be in tune with ourselves we should acknowledge the difference and live it. Prayer times, structured by or inspired by the Advent Readings, can fit into this time of year in a very natural manner.

Advent Carol Services
The commercial world begins Christmas long before the Church begins Advent, and it closes the season on December 26. But the wall-to-wall Christmas music in supermarkets and

shopping centres is in reality just a stimulus aimed at triggering off nostalgic responses (most of which have to do with digging deeper into pockets and purses!), and has no overt religious significance at all.

This presents us with a certain problem. People tend to be fed up of Christmas music before Christmas comes at all, and a frequent response is to put on a Carol Service early in Advent, before excessive boredom sets in. There is also the very real problem that a torpor settles over parishes after Christmas Day and people don't come together to celebrate the Nativity after the Feast itself. What is the solution? Certainly not a refusal to hold such services during Advent! Much more constructive would be an attempt to emphasise the Advent themes in songs and readings — themes which in any case are more solid and challenging than the usually sterile sentimentality of the traditional Carol Service.

It is a question of orientation and emphasis. One should retain what is appealing about the Carol Service format: a fairly fixed and predictable structure within which variants may be inserted, a dignity of language in biddings and prayers, a good balance between music for all and special pieces for choirs or folk-groups, a carefully prepared setting with suitable atmosphere. Within this structure, readings, mimes, dramas can take their place. These should embrace not just the history of the chosen people and the historical preparation for the birth of Christ, but also the Advent longings of all peoples and civilisations. All situations of expectancy, of yearning for fulness of life, can be used to illustrate the themes of the season.

As in the Advent Liturgy of the Hours the whole celebration should leave people with the keen consciousness that the Advent of Christ is happening now, to us, and that through us it is going to happen to others if it happens at all. This is the ultimate fruit of the Advent Office, of Advent spirituality. Only in this way, through this commitment, can the true light shine on us, the light of God's promise in our feeble half-light:

All out of darkness we have light,
which made the angels sing this night.

And that's a song worth singing!

1. Laurence Mayer and Alan Scheible, *Evening Prayer in the Parish,* Chicago, Liturgy Publications, 1981, 2.
2. This theme is extensively dealt with in Paul Ricouer, *The Symbolism of Evil,* Boston, Beacon Press, 1969.
3. Brendan Purcell, *In Search of Newgrange: Long Night's Journey into Day,* in *The Irish Mind,* ed. Richard Kearney, Dublin, Wolfhound Press, 1985,55.
4. In the sense in which Bruce Marshall took it as the title of one of his novels: that pettiness and cant may be transfigured by grace. The phrase is, of course, taken from Ps 45:13.
5. This 'Matin Responsory' is very popular in Advent Carol Services, and is sung to an adapted Palestrina 'Magnificat': see *Carols for Choirs 2* (edited by David Willcocks and John Rutter, Oxford University press 1970), 68-70.
6. The chief texts used are Is 45:8; 64:6-7; 16:1; 43:1-3 and 54:4-8.
7. The history and theology of this hymn is dealt with in Frank Colquhoun's *Hymns that Live* (London, Hodder & Stoughton, 1980), 32-37.
8. London, SPCK, 1982.
9. London and New York, Sheed and Ward, 1951. The piece on the 'The Rod of Jesse' (pages 7-8) is particularly fine.

The Weekdays of Advent

Timothy O'Connor

The main themes of Advent are presented in the readings from Sacred Scripture for the four Sundays: Vigilance in preparation for the second coming of the Lord; Preparing the way of the Lord; The joy of the Messianic times; Preparing for the birth of the Saviour. These great themes are developed and expanded in the readings for the weekdays according to the two main divisions of the season: Advent I with the emphasis on the second coming of the Lord (weeks 1-3) and Advent II with the emphasis on the birth of Jesus. But the liturgy does not adhere rigidly to this division. It is rather like a symphony where future themes are introduced early on to be fully developed later, with a constant interweaving of snatches now of one theme and then of another. What the liturgy does is to integrate the two major aspects of the season, the second coming of the Lord and his first coming, in a way that stresses the dependence of the one on the other.

The readings for the season are taken from those bible authors who best describe the eschatological nature of the Christian pilgrimage, with frequent correspondence between the Gospel reading and that from the Old Testament. It is these readings that give us the themes. Then it is the meditation and prayer texts that help us to assimilate and make personal the themes in our lives. The sources of our study are the texts from the lectionary and Missal and those of the Liturgy of the Hours.

The dominant Christian attitude of the Advent season is hope, giving us a confident Christian messianism which builds up a community of salvation and hope. But the pre-requisite for this is faith and while awaiting the second coming the Christian must live a life of love.

The first week of Advent
Awaiting the second coming of the Lord

1. The end result of the second coming will be the gathering together of the scattered people of God. This is the ultimate and the chief work of Jesus. 'All nations will stream to the mountain of the Temple of the Lord' (Isaiah, Monday), and 'many will come from the east and west to take their places with Abraham and Isaac and Jacob at the feast in the kingdom of heaven' (Matthew, Monday). With the restoration of unity to the human family all creation will be restored, with peace, as people walk in the light of the Lord. The judgement of the Lord is to be seen in a positive light as ushering in an era of justice, peace and renewal (Liturgy of the Hours, Tuesday).

2. It is the Lord Jesus who brings all this to pass. He does this in virtue of the Spirit of the Lord who rests on him, 'a spirit of wisdom and insight, a spirit of counsel and power, a spirit of knowledge and of the fear of the Lord' (Isaiah, Tuesday). To him everything 'has been entrusted by his Father'; 'no one knows who the Son is except the Father, and who the Father is except the Son and those to whom the Son chooses to reveal him' (Luke, Wednesday). This is summed up in the entrance song: 'See, the Lord is coming and with him all his saints. Then there will be endless day' (Tuesday).

3. The source of this restoration is the goodness of the Lord. 'He will be gracious to you when he hears your cry; when he hears he will answer . . . The Lord dresses the wounds of his people and heals the bruises his blows have left' (Isaiah, Saturday). And the Lord Jesus "felt sorry for the crowds because they were harassed and dejected, like sheep without a shepherd" (Matthew, Saturday). And so the opening prayer asserts that "God loved the world so much

that he gave his only Son to free us from the ancient power of sin and death' and prays: 'Help us who wait for his coming and lead us to true liberty'.

4. Already the signs of the kingdom and its first-fruits are among us. This is one of the characteristics of Advent hope — that we already have what we hope for. The second coming will establish for all time what we have now in embryonic form. The signs of the kingdom among us are: (a) Sight to the blind. This means much more than the giving of physical sight to the blind for it pre-supposes faith and is a symbol of the insight into the mysteries of the kingdom which the believer is capable of. Isaiah makes it a mark of the restored universe: "That day the eyes of the blind will see" (Friday) and the Gospel of the same day shows the fulfilment in the present messianic times: 'Your faith deserves it . . . and their sight returned'(Matthew 9). (b) The compassion of the Lord is foretold by Isaiah (Saturday) and realised by Jesus in his own activity and in the mission given to the apostles (Gospel, Saturday). (c) The Banquet of the Lord is the symbol of the harmony and the unity of the assembled people of God in the kingdom. This banquet is indicated by the multiplication of the loaves by Jesus, a sign of the Eucharist which is 'the pledge of future glory' (Isaiah, Wednesday; Gospel, Wednesday). So, we pray on Wednesday: 'Grant that we may be ready to receive Christ when he comes in glory and to share in the banquet of heaven'.

5. All this requires a conversion (Liturgy of the Hours. Wednesday), a life that is just: 'Let the upright nation come in, she the faithful one, whose mind is steadfast, who keeps the peace' (Isaiah Thursday) and fidelity to God's will: 'The person who does the will of my Father in heaven will enter the kingdom of heaven' (Gospel, Thursday). That means that the people of God must work at building the kingdom on earth to ensure their place in the kingdom at the end of time. It is for this dynamic between earth and heaven that we pray on Friday: 'Father, you give us

food from heaven. By our sharing in this mystery, teach us to judge wisely the things of earth and to love the things of heaven.'

6. The exaltation of Mount Sion is the theme running through the readings of the Liturgy of the Hours for this week. 'The vineyard of the Lord of hosts is the house of Israel and the men of Judah are his pleasant planting' (Wednesday) but it must be converted. Sion will be the centre of the eschatological kingdom, but it is a symbolic Jerusalem which the prophet describes, detached from history and geography, a spiritual, universal Sion open to all peoples who are called to assembly for its liturgy (Monday; Thursday). This is the vision of the kingdom of the future. In the Patristic readings of the Liturgy of the Hours the message of the Scriptures is developed with exhortation on living in expectation of the coming of the Lord. 'He said that he will come again but he did not say exactly when. Hence, all generations and ages live in eager expectation of him. The Lord pointed out the signs of his coming but we have no knowledge of when they will be completed. In many varied ways they have happened and passed away and are still happening. His last coming is in fact like his first . . . Be on the watch' (St Ephraem, Thursday). 'Waiting and patience are necessary if we are to fulfil what we have begun to be, and to receive, through God's unfailing help, what we hope for and believe' (St Cyprian, Saturday). Perhaps it is St Bernard who fully captures the spirit and meaning of Advent in the Wednesday reading: 'We have come to know a threefold coming of the Lord. The third coming takes place between the other two. In the first coming the Lord was seen on earth and lived among men . . . In his last coming all flesh shall see the salvation of our God. The other coming is hidden. In it, only the chosen see him within themselves and their souls are saved. This intermediary coming is like a road leading from the first to the last coming during which the words of God are to be kept in the heart' (Wednesday).

The Second Week of Advent
Prepare the way of the Lord

This week the Lord who is to come is a gracious Lord who saves, who consoles, gives strength to the weary as he listens to their cries.

1. *I, the Holy One of Israel, am your redeemer* (Isaiah)
'For I, the Lord, your God, I am holding you by the right hand; I tell you, do not be afraid, I will help you' (Thursday).
Your God is coming to save you (Isaiah)
'They will come to Zion shouting for joy, everlasting joy on their faces; joy and gladness will go with them and sorrow and lament be ended' (Monday).
Console my people, console them (Isaiah)
'Speak to the heart of Jerusalem and call to her that her time of service is ended, that her sin is atoned for' (Tuesday).
He gives strength to the weary, he strengthens the powerless (Isaiah)
'Those who hope in the Lord renew their strength, they put out wings like eagles. They run and do not grow weary, walk and never tire' (Wednesday).

2. The Lord Jesus fulfills these prophecies, in the messianic age:
   He forgives sins and tells the paralytic to 'get up and walk' (Monday).
   Nobody is outside his concern. 'It is never the will of your Father in heaven that one of these little ones should be lost' (Tuesday).
   His invitation is: 'Come to me all you who labour and are overburdened, and I will give you rest' (Wednesday).

3. 'The prophet Elijah arose like a fire, his word flaring like a torch' says Sirach. His function is to 'turn the hearts of fathers towards children and to restore the tribe of Jacob',

to bring people into unity, to reassemble, exactly what will happen in the second coming. Elijah will come again. But he did come in the person of John the Baptist: 'I tell you that Elijah has come already and they did not recognise him' (Gospel, Saturday). John the Baptist was the greatest of the prophets (Thursday) but not only did they not listen to him, they refused to listen to the very Son himself. One must recognise the Lord's coming in his envoys if one is to be accepted at his second coming and put oneself in the plan of reconstruction by observing the commandments (Isaiah, Friday). It is the violent who will take the kingdom by storm (Gospel, Friday). That is the kingdom described in Psalm 144 (Thursday), a kingdom of glory, of might, and splendour which will last for ever. The way to prepare for his coming is to 'Let our lives be honest and holy in this present age, as we wait for the happiness to come when our great God reveals himself in glory' (Communion Chant, Thursday).

In the Liturgy of the Hours for this second week the events of the last days, the days of judgement are predominant.

A pathetic image of the earth is depicted, a 'scorched earth with few men left . . . the gladness of the earth is banished with desolation left in the city . . . the windows of heaven are opened and foundations of the earth tremble (Isaiah, Monday). Yet the responsory to that reading is full of joy: 'They lift up their voices, they sing for joy; in the east give glory to the Lord'. Indeed, the description of destruction at the end of time is very rare in the Advent liturgy which is extremely positive and hopeful. There will be judgement, certainly, but 'strong people will glorify you . . . you have been a stronghold to the poor, a stronghold to the needy in his distress' (Isaiah, Tuesday).

The great Messianic banquet is the lot of all those who are faithful to their God. It is a glorious affirmation of the reward of patient fidelity. 'We have waited for him that he might save us . . . let us be glad and rejoice in his salvation' and the great song of the redeemed bursts from grateful hearts (Isaiah, Wednesday). It is righteousness that leads to this happy state, which is none other than resurrection: 'Your dead shall live, their bodies shall rise' (Isaiah, Thursday). The Lord guards his vineyard lest any one harm it; it is the renewal of Jerusalem, a new spiritual Jerusalem, which will be the final assembly place of the faithful remnant who will worship the Lord on his holy mountain (Isaiah, Friday).

The second reading of the Liturgy of the Hours, quoting 'Lumen Gentium' puts the Church in the context of the assembly of the remnant in the new Jerusalem and, looking forward to the second great theme of Advent, relate the place of Mary in that Church. 'The Church, to which we are all called in Christ Jesus, and in which we acquire sanctity through the grace of God, will attain her full perfection only in the glory of heaven. Then will come the time of the restoration of all things. Then the human race, as well as the entire world, which is intimately related to man and achieves its purpose through him, will be perfectly re-established in Christ' (Lumen Gentium, Tuesday). That locates us in the whole perspective of Isaiah and Jesus in the Gospel of these days. Isaac of Stella does the same for Mary (Saturday). 'Each is mother, each is virgin; both conceived in holiness from the same Spirit; both bring forth a child without sin for God, the Father. Mary gave birth to the absolutely sinless Head for the Body; the Church gave birth, in the forgiveness of every sin, to the Body for the Head. Each is the mother of Christ, but neither without the other gives birth to the whole Christ.'

Finally, St John of the Cross tells us where to find our centre in this life so as to achieve our fulfilment in the next: The Father speaks: 'Already with my Holy Spirit, I descended on him on Mount Thabor and said, "This is my beloved Son, with whom I am well pleased; listen to him". Hear him, because I have no more faith to reveal or anything to manifest. If I spoke in former times it was to promise Christ. And if they questioned me, their requests were steps along the road to want Christ and hope for him in whom they were to find all that is good. This is now confirmed by everything the apostles and evangelists teach' (Monday).

The Third Week of Advent
Messianic Longing and Fulfilment

In the liturgy of the third week of Advent the Old Testament vision of the messianic times and the New Testament fulfilment in Jesus, the Messiah, becomes a personalised and individual acceptance or rejection of God's salvation with a commitment that demands every effort of a person's spirit. All this is to be seen and understood against the background of strong emphasis on the second coming of Jesus, the Messiah. Thus, the past, the present and the future, so inextricably linked in Advent thought, are here bound together through the living out of messianic hopes in a person; for ultimately that is where it must take root, but in persons linked together by the same messianic hope, a hope that will prove victorious.

The prophecy of Balaam (Monday), 'A start from Jacob takes the leadership', is seen fulfilled in Jesus who asserts his leadership and authority, particularly through his healing and deliverance and through his authoritative affirmation of John the Baptist. Though he does not declare the source of his authority he clearly implies where it comes from (Gospel, Monday). Zephaniah sees messianic salvation promised to all the poor in spirit: 'In your midst I will leave a humble and lowly people and those who are left in Israel will seek refuge in the name of the Lord' (Zephaniah, Tuesday). God's relationship with his people is personal and intimate: 'Like a forsaken wife, distressed in spirit, the Lord calls you back . . . . my love for you will never leave you' (Isaiah, Thursday). This intimate relationship will be the lot of foreigners too, so that God's friendship is universal and unlimited: 'Foreigners who have attached themselves to the Lord to serve him — I will make them joyful in my house of prayer' (Isaiah,

Friday). With this assurance, expressed in such personal terms, the great prayer of desire and longing reaches out to God: 'Send victory like a dew, you heavens, and let the clouds rain it down. Let the earth open for salvation to spring up. Turn to me and be saved . . . victorious and glorious through the Lord shall be all the descendants of Israel' (Isaiah, Wednesday). This is the Advent theme-prayer, the core of man's longing for deliverance, giving us the splendid Advent antiphon, 'Rorate Caeli desuper et nubes pluant justum" recurring as a motif through the whole liturgy of the season.

Jesus Messiah is the fulfilment of all these promises. His assurance to John's messengers is that the prophecies have been fulfilled in him and particularly in his acts of healing, caring and deliverance. John the Baptist would know that these were foretold and would now know that they became a reality in the person of Jesus Christ Messiah (Gospel, Wednesday).

John the Baptist is more than a prophet; he is the one who announces and prepares for the imminent fulfilment of all that the Old Testament has foretold. He did this not only by his preaching but by his life. Acceptance of prophecies meant acceptance that one's life is to be lived in the spirit of these prophecies. So 'John came as a pattern of true righteousness': there is 'no one greater than John': he gave 'testimony to the truth . . . he was a lamp alight and shining'. He was humble, self-effacing, true to his mission. Those who were humble and sincere 'acknowledged God's plan by accepting baptism from John', but the Pharisees and the lawyers refused to accept his baptism and so 'had thwarted what God had in mind for them' (Gospel, Friday). 'John came to you, a pattern of true righteousness, but you did not believe him' (Gospel, Tuesday). Personal acceptance and conversion is demanded of everybody and John gave the lead, being faithful unto death. All this must lead ultimately to the full acceptance of Jesus in whom all the promises are centred and completed: 'My testimony is greater than John's: the works my Father has given me to carry out, these same works of mine testify that the Father has sent me' (Gospel, Friday).

Christ completes the whole of revelation (Second Reading, Thursday). 'Jesus Christ, sent as a man among men, speaks the words of God, and accomplishes the saving work which the Father gave him to do. As a result, he himself completed and perfected revelation and confirmed it with divine guarantees. He did this by the total fact of his presence and self-manifestation — by words and works, signs and miracles, but above all by his death and glorious resurrection from the dead, and finally by sending the Spirit of truth. He revealed that God was with us, to deliver us from the darkness of sin and death, and to raise us up to eternal life' (Constitution on Divine Revelation). St Irenaeus (Liturgy of Hours, Second Reading, Wednesday), describes God's plan in this way: 'For the Word of God foretold from the beginning that God would be seen by men and would live with them on earth and converse with them; that he would be present with his creatures to bring salvation to them and to be perceived by them; that he would free us from the hands of those who hate us, that is, from the whole spirit of transgression; and would make us serve him all our days in holiness and righteousness; that man, taking to himself the Spirit of God, would pass to the glory of the Father.' As desire and longing is the characteristic attitude of soul for Advent, St Augustine tells how this is to be expressed in prayer (Liturgy of the Hours, Second Reading, Friday): 'There is another and interior way of praying without ceasing, and that is the way of desire. Whatever else you are doing, if you long for that sabbath, you are not ceasing to pray. If you do not want to cease praying, do not cease longing. Your unceasing desire is your unceasing voice. You will lapse into silence if you lose your longing' (Discourse on the Psalms).

It is the biblical readings of the Liturgy of the Hours that give the eschatological dimension to the third week: conversion and future happiness (Monday). The coming of the Lord will inaugurate a reign of justice (Wednesday), a restoration

(Thursday) giving rise to hope (Thursday). This is the future salvation (Friday) and there is a warning of chastisement for those who will not accept God's favours (Tuesday).

The prayers of the liturgy of this week ask that we recognise the presence of Jesus among us and give him entry into our heart and allow him to save us: e.g. 'Father of love, you made a new creation through Jesus Christ your Son. May his coming free us from sin and renew his life within us' (Collect, Tuesday).

The Fourth Week of Advent.
The Word Made Flesh

During this fourth week each day brings us into a deeper appreciation and understanding of the imminent mystery of the Incarnation. The readings interpret the mystery for us; the chants allow our spirits to sing out in joyful expectation while the prayer texts express our intense desire (as St Augustine encouraged us to do last week) to bring the mystery into our very lives.

December 17: St Matthew by his genealogy shows how Christ is inserted into human history, and into the history of Judah, being the son of David, thus ensuring that the 'sceptre will not pass from Judah' (First Reading). St Leo comments (Second Reading, Liturgy of Hours): 'Matthew says: The book of the genealogy of Jesus Christ, son of David, the son of Abraham. He then follows the order of Christ's human origin and traces the line of his ancestry down to Joseph, to whom the Lord's mother was betrothed'; and he expresses the deep meaning of this human lineage in a beautiful passage: 'If the new man, made in the likeness of sinful flesh, had not taken our old nature; if he, one in substance with the Father, had not accepted to be one in substance with the mother; if he who was alone free from sin had not united our nature to himself, then men would still have been held captive under the power of the devil. We would have been incapable of profiting by the victor's triumph if the battle had been fought outside our nature.' So we pray that the incarnate Word may take our human nature and make it share in his divinity: 'Grant that the Word who took flesh in the womb of the ever-virgin Mary and became a man like us, may share with us his godhead' (Collect). And we pray in the intercessions: 'Born of a woman, you will open in our flesh the way to eternal life and joy. Come, Lord Jesus, do not delay.'

December 18: The Word will be made flesh in the womb of the Virgin Mary, by the power of the Holy Spirit; he will save his people from their sins, as indicated by his name, Jesus; and this is the fulfilment of the specific prophecy of Isaiah: 'The virgin will conceive and give birth to a son and they will call him Emmanuel, a name which means "God-is-with us" (Gospel). He is the one who will establish justice and integrity (First Reading). 'In his days justice shall flourish and peace till the moon falls' (Response).

That we needed the saviour to free us from sin is expressed by the epistle to Diognetus: 'He was preparing this present era of righteousness. His purpose was that we, who in those days had been proved by our own works unworthy to achieve life, might in these days be made worthy of it by the goodness of God. After clearly showing our inability to enter into the kingdom of God by our own power, we might now by God's power be made able.' And so we pray: 'by the long-awaited coming of your new-born Son, deliver us, Lord, from the age-old bondage of sin'. We want Jesus to save us from our sins and to cooperate with him in bringing his justice to the world: 'For the work man must do in creating a more just world, make our hearts ready, O Lord.'

December 19 and 23: The birth of John the Baptist is so important that it is proclaimed twice this week. God makes a free choice of his agents; he gives a special name; he makes a special announcement, received by Zachary with disbelief (unlike Mary who believed). God intervenes in a special way to choose his agents — Isaac, Jacob, Moses, John the Baptist. The first reading of December 19 shows the parallel between the conception of John and that of Samson. Nothing is impossible to God and he shows his favour in spectacular ways. So the responsorial psalm sings: 'It is you, O Lord, who are my hope, my trust, O Lord, since my youth. On you I have leaned from my birth, from my mother's womb you have been my help.' At his birth, when Zachary has recovered his speech, the people ask: "What will this child turn out to be? . . . as indeed the hand of the Lord was with him' (Gospel, December 23). He will be Elijah come back to earth as foretold by Malachi and confirmed by Jesus, himself. We pray: 'The Baptist preached a change of heart, free us from self-satisfaction' and "The Baptist was glad to make way for him, free us from pride" (Intercessions, December 23).

December 20, 21 and 22: In these days Mary takes her place among the other 'watchers' of Advent — Isaiah and John the Baptist. We realise that she is mentioned and celebrated throughout Advent; she appears in these last days because no one expects as much as the expectant mother who became so completely a part of the plan of God. So, we have (1) 'You will conceive and bear a Son' (Gospel, December 20), (2) 'Mary set out at that time and went as quickly as she could to a town in the hill country of Judah', (3) 'The Almighty has done great things for me' — her song of praise is the Gospel for December 22. Each of these texts from St Luke is introduced by a first reading which is a distinct parallel from the Old Testament. Thus: (1) The prophecy of Isaiah, 'A virgin will conceive' (December 20), 'I hear my Beloved. See how he comes leaping on the mountains, bounding over the hills' (December 21) from Canticle of Canticles and (3) 'This is the child I prayed for, and the Lord granted me what I asked him. Now, I make him over to the Lord for the whole of his life' — the thanks of Hannah from the first book of Samuel. The joy of the Church, waiting with Mary is expressed in the Liturgy of the Hours in antiphons of great lyric beauty and filled with holy emotion. The antiphons for Prayer during the Day are all Marian antiphons based on the Gospel readings of the Mass. The responsories, too, always reflect the Marian aspect. We have, too, some of the great patristic commentaries on the gospel of St Luke: e.g. St Leo on December 17; St Irenaeus, 'Against the Heresies' on December 19; St Ambrose on December 21, 'Where could she who was filled with God hasten to, except to the heights? There is no such thing as delay in the working of the Holy Spirit. The arrival of Mary and the blessings of the Lord's presence are also speedily declared . . . Let the soul of Mary be in each one of you to magnify the Lord. Let the spirit of Mary be in each one to exult in God'. St Bede comments on the 'Magnificat' on December 22; and the most beautiful of all is found on December 20 when St Bernard has the whole world in suspense, waiting for the consent of the Virgin Mother: 'On your lips is hanging the consolation of the wretched, the redemption of the captive, the speedy deliverance of all who otherwise are lost; in a word, the salvation of all Adam's children, of all your races'. So, Advent is a Marian season — with the feast of the Immaculate Conception, too, in Advent, though to be seen in the full context of the complete Marian doctrine portrayed in Advent. We should go to Advent for the sure basis of our Marian devotion, the expression of the authentic voice of the bible and tradition.

It is interesting to note that in the biblical readings of the Liturgy of the Hours it is, once again, the eschatological aspect that dominates: the salvation of Israel through King Cyrus (December 17); The God of Israel destroys the idols of the nations (December 18); Lament for fallen Babylon (December 19); God acts alone and is sole Master of the future (December 20); The new Exodus (December 20); The restoration of Zion (December 22); The promise of salvation to the children of Abraham. Thus, despite the imminence of the birth of Jesus Messiah, we are never allowed to forget the tension that always exists between messianic times now and the restoration and accomplishment of all things in the Parousia.

Celebrating Advent with Children

Maura Hyland

Because of the anticipation and joy with which children await Christmas, it is relatively easy to help them come to some understanding of the Advent themes of waiting, preparing, looking forward. This chapter gives some examples of children's prayer liturgies for Advent, as well as directions for the use of the Advent wreath and the Jesse tree.

There are other and equally important activities which children love and which help them to find ways of expressing their sense of excitement at the coming of Christmas:
— decorating the room
— making a crib and crib figures
— making Christmas cards
— exploring the origins of Christmas customs
— learning carols
— planning how they will spend Christmas day
— thinking of visiting or giving a gift to someone, perhaps an old person, for whom Christmas may be a lonely time.
— thinking of New Year resolutions.

A Prayerservice for Advent (4-8 year olds)

All: Sign of the Cross.
Leader: During the four weeks before Christmas we are waiting to celebrate the birthday of Jesus. Often we have to wait to celebrate an important happening in our family — a birthday, a wedding, a baptism. While we wait for Christmas, we think of those who waited for the first Christmas. We think especially of Mary, the mother of Jesus, of the preparations she

made, of the hopes she had and of the joy she felt when Jesus was born.

Let us ask God to help us to prepare for this Christmas as well as Mary prepared for the first Christmas.

Child: God our Father, help us to bring the joy and happiness which Mary felt on the first Christmas night, to the people who will be with us this Christmas.

All: 'Thank you, God, for Jesus,' is the prayer we say.

Child: God our Father, help us to bring happiness to someone who is lonely this Christmas, to an old person who lives nearby or to someone who won't get many presents.

All: 'Thank you, God, for Jesus,' is the prayer we say.

Child: God our Father, help us to think of others before ourselves this Christmas.

All: 'Thank you, God, for Jesus,' is the prayer we say.

Child: God our Father, when we give presents this Christmas, help us to remember that the most important gift of all is love. Help us to give the gift of love to our family and friends this Christmas.

All: 'Thank you, God, for Jesus,' is the prayer we say.

Leader: Let us thank God together for sending Jesus into the world on the first Christmas night.

All: 'Thank you, God, for Jesus,'
is the prayer we say.
'Thank you, God, for Jesus,
born on Christmas Day.'

A Penance Service for Advent (6-8 year olds)

Opening
Hymn: We have come to say sorry.

All: Sign of the Cross.

Leader: Everywhere we see people preparing for Christmas. They are buying presents, decorating the house, icing the cake, searching for a suitable Christmas tree. In the towns and cities there are bright lights in the streets and the shop windows are full of brightly wrapped presents. Today we are going to prepare our hearts for the coming of Jesus. Before Jesus was born, God sent a messenger called John to tell them how to prepare for his coming. This is what John told the people:

Reader: The Lord be with you.

All: And also with you.

Reader: A reading from the Holy Gospel according to Luke.

All: Glory to you, Lord.

Reader: Share everything you have with others, especially with those who have nothing. Don't treat anybody unfairly. Don't take anything that you don't have a right to. Don't bully anybody. Don't tell lies.
(Luke 3:10-14 adapted)

Examination of conscience

Leader: When Jesus was on earth, he showed us how to share with others, how to be kind and loving of all those around us, how to be fair and how to think especially of those who are in most need of help. Let us ask ourselves if we have been living as Jesus showed us.

Have you shown your parents that you love them by doing what they ask you?

Pause

Have you shown your friends at school that you love them by sharing your toys and your books with them, and by helping them when they find things too difficult?

Pause

Have you ever taken anything that did not belong to you and kept it for yourself?

Pause

Have you shown your friends at playtime that you love them by playing fairly, by not bullying, by not being angry or bad-tempered?

Pause

124

Have you shown God our Father that you love him by remembering to say your prayers and to thank him for his gifts?
Pause

Act of Repentance

Leader: Let us confess that we have not lived as Jesus showed us.

All: Confiteor.

Child: If there were times when we did not do as our mammies and daddies asked us,

All: We are sorry.

Child: If there were times when we didn't share our toys or our books with our friends,

All: We are sorry.

Child: If there were times when we took things that didn't belong to us,

All: We are sorry.

Child: If there were times when we were unfair, when we bullied others or were angry or bad-tempered,

All: We are sorry.

Child: If there were times when we forgot to say our prayers,

All: We are sorry.

Leader: Let us pray the Act of Sorrow:
O my God, thank you for loving me.
I am sorry for all my sins,
for not loving others and for not loving you.
Help me to live like Jesus and not sin again. Amen.

Leader: Jesus told us that when we say sorry and try again, God our Father will always forgive us. Let us make up our minds to try again as we say together the prayer that Jesus taught his friends:

All: Our Father

Final Blessing

Leader: Go in peace to live as Jesus showed us.

All: Amen.

Leader: Go in peace to bring love to all those we live and play with.

All: Amen.

Leader: May almighty God bless us all, Father, Son and Holy Spirit.

All: Amen.

Final Hymn: I am sorry, God.

A Prayerservice for Advent (8-12 year olds)

All: Sign of the Cross

Leader: During Advent we look forward to Christmas. Christmas is a time of happiness and joy because at Christmas we celebrate the fact that God has sent his son, Jesus, into the world to show us how to live and how to love. For four thousand years the people longed for the coming of Jesus. The prophets helped them to prepare for his coming. For nine months his mother, Mary, waited for the birth of her son. During the four weeks of Advent, we try to prepare our hearts for the coming of Jesus at Christmas. Let us listen to the promise of the coming of Jesus in the words of John the Baptist:

Reader: 'A stronger one than I comes after me,' John told the people. 'I am not good enough to bend down and untie his shoe-laces.' ('*New World*', Alan T Dale, Oxford)

Child: The coming of Jesus at Christmas is a gift of love. God showed us the great love he had for us by sending his son into the world on the first Christmas night.

Child: God our Father, help us to bring the gift of love to all those we meet this Christmas, to our parents and our family, to our friends at school and at play, to the people in our neighbourhood.

All: Blessed be the Lord, the God of Israel, because he has visited his people and redeemed them.

Child: The coming of Jesus at Christmas is a challenge to us to respond in our lives to the love God has shown to us at Christmas.

Child: God our Father, help us to show our love for you by showing love to those around us, to our parents and our family at home, to our friends in school and at play and to the people in our community.

All: Blessed be the Lord, the God of Israel, because he has visited his people and redeemed them.

Encourage the children to add their own reflections and prayers.

Leader: May the Lord be with us to guide us as we prepare for the coming of Jesus this Christmas.

All: Amen.

A Penance Service for Advent (8-12 year olds)

Preparation: Put a lighted candle in the centre of the group, on a table or in a candle holder.

All: Sign of the Cross.

Leader: Peace be with you.

All: And also with you.

Leader: Today we have come to pause for a little while and to think of the many ways in which we have failed to live in the way God asks us. As we prepare for Christmas, we remember again God's great love for us which is most clearly shown in the coming of his son, Jesus. We ask for his forgiveness and his help as we promise to do our best to try again in the future. Let us listen again to the command of Jesus:

Reader: The Lord be with you.

All: And also with you.

Reader: A reading from the Holy Gospel according to John.

All: Glory to you, Lord.

Reader: This is my commandment, love one another as I have loved you . . . You are my friends if you do as I command . . . The command I give you is this, that you love one another. (*John 15:12,14,17.*)

Examination of conscience

We refuse to love others as Jesus asks when we don't do as we are told by our parents or by our teachers.

Did you fail to do as you were told?

Pause

We refuse to love others as Jesus asks when we lose our tempers and quarrel and fight with others.

Did you lose your temper?

Pause

We refuse to love others as Jesus asks when we give bad example.

Did you give bad example?

Pause

We refuse to love as Jesus asks when we are selfish and refuse to share our toys or our books or our sweets with others.

Did you refuse to share with others?

Pause

We refuse to love as Jesus asks when we are careless about saying our prayers, or when we don't pay attention or distract others at Mass.

Have you been careless about your prayers?

Pause

We refuse to love as Jesus asks when we swear or call names.

Did you swear or call names?

Pause

We refuse to love as Jesus asks when we tell lies.

Did you tell lies?

Pause

We refuse to love as Jesus asks when we are dishonest, when we take or keep things that don't belong to us.

128

Did you take or keep anything that didn't belong to you?
Pause

Act of Repentance
Leader: Together let us confess that we have sinned.
All: Confiteor.
Leader: Let us ask for forgiveness for the times when we have failed:
Child: If there were times when we didn't do as we were told,
All: Lord, have mercy.
Child: If there were times when we lost our tempers or got angry,
All: Lord, have mercy.
Child: If there were times when we gave bad example,
All: Lord, have mercy.
Child: If there were times when we refused to share with others,
All: Lord, have mercy.
Child: If there were times when we were careless about our prayers.
All: Lord, have mercy.
Child: If there were times when we swore or called names,
All: Lord, have mercy.
Child: If there were times when we told lies,
All: Lord, have mercy.
Child: If there were times when we were dishonest,
All: Lord, have mercy.
Leader: Together let us say the Act of Sorrow:
O my God, I thank you for loving me.
I am sorry for all my sins,
for not loving others and not loving you.
Help me to live like Jesus and not sin again.

The leader invites the children to write their own resolutions for the future. The leader also writes his or her own resolution and they are all placed around the candle.

Leader: Let us pray together in the words Jesus taught us:
All: Our Father

Final Blessing
Leader: Go in peace to love one another as Jesus taught.
All: Amen.
Leader: Go in peace to build a better world.
All: Amen.
Leader: Go in peace to be a light for the world.
All: Amen.
Leader: May almighty God bless us all, Father, Son and Holy Spirit.
All: Amen.

The Advent wreath

The Advent wreath takes up the Christmas theme of light. 'Whatever came to be in him, found life, life for the light of men. The light shines in the darkness, a darkness that did not overcome it.' (*John 1:4-5*)

To make the wreath, you first form a circle of wire. Clothes hangers are excellent and the right size for classroom or home use. The circle represents the coming of Christ on the first Christmas night, his coming in our hearts this Christmas and his final coming at the end of the world. Evergreens are twined around the wire circle, using string or wire to hold them in place. Green is the Church's sign of hope. Into the circle are now fixed four candles, three of them purple and one rose-coloured. The purple candles represent the Church's call to conversion during Advent and the rose candle represents our joy at the approach of Christmas. The wreath may be decorated with a red ribbon.

During the first week of Advent, one candle is lit during prayertime, two during the second week and so on. The rose coloured candle is lit during the third week.

On the first day of each week, when the new candle is to be lit for the first time, a new prayer is said. The following is an example, but as Advent progresses it would be good to encourage the children to compose their own prayers.

Lighting of the candles
All :   Sign of the Cross
Leader: As we prepare to light this candle, we remember once again that we are waiting for the coming of Christ this Christmas. We remember that on the first Christmas night Jesus brought light into the world, a light to show people how to live and how to love. We pray that that same light will come into our hearts this Christmas.
A child lights the candles and says: God our Father, as we prepare for Christmas, send the light of Christ into our hearts to show us how to love others and how to love you.
All: Amen.

Suitable hymns could also be added in.

The Jesse tree

The Jesse tree is based on the family tree idea and its biblical roots are in the text from Isaiah 11:7: 'A shoot shall sprout from the stump of Jesse and from his roots a bud shall blossom'. The following approach to the Jesse tree is usable with 11-12 year olds.

To make the tree a very large branch from a leafless tree is placed upright in a bucket or large box and made secure with sand or stones. Alternatively a tree shape can be cut out of white paper and pasted on a black background. The tree is then decorated with symbols of Jesus' ancestors and events or happenings in their lives. Groups of children could take turns at providing the symbols and finding the biblical texts which explain the symbols. One symbol could be added each day during Advent.

The following are some examples which are connected with biblical characters and themes with which the children should be familiar:

131

Creation	Genesis 1:1-2,2.	World; sun, stars, animals, plants etc
Abraham	Genesis 12:5	Shepherd's crook
Joseph	Genesis 37:2-36	coloured coat, sheaf of wheat
Moses	Exodus 2:1-10	basket, commandments on stone tablets
Ruth	Ruth 1:1-22	sheaf of wheat
David	1 Samuel 16:1-13	oil
Solomon	1 Kings 3:16-28	scales
Elizabeth	Luke 1:39-45	old woman with baby
Zechariah	Luke 1:5-25	burning incense
John the Baptist	Matthew 1:18-25	carpenter's tools
Mary	Mark 3:31-25	young woman with baby
Shepherds	Luke 2:8-20	sheep, shepherd's staff
Wise Men	Matthew 2:1-12	gifts, star, camel.

The final symbol is the Chi-Rho (☧) and it is placed on the topmost branch on the last schoolday before Christmas.

The symbols can be drawn and cut out of white card or paper and hung on the tree or pasted onto the black background.

The above are only suggestions. It is likely that the children themselves would be very interested in thinking up their own symbols, based on their knowledge of the story in question. This would be an even better learning experience.

For older children, especially in secondary schools, a selection of suitable prayerservices can be found in *Prayerservices for Young People* by Donal Neary SJ (Columba Press 1985) and suitable Penance Services are available in *Penitential Services,* edited by Oliver Crilly (Columba Press 1986).

Advent Imagery and Symbols

Genevieve Mooney OP

Advent is a season rich in imagery and symbol, but the greatest symbol in the whole celebration is Advent itself. In itself it is symbolic. It has multiple meanings at many levels. There is more to it than is readily evident or can be grasped and analysed rationally. It is not an arbitrary liturgical period prescribed by the Church. If it were not given to us, we would invent it in some form. In the northern hemisphere it corresponds to a season of nature's yearly cycle, has its roots in this and draws great strength and power from it. Everywhere it corresponds to a part of human experience, a recurring season in human life — the ambivalence of rejoicing in the 'already' while longing for the 'not yet' and a reaching out from the very depths of us towards wholeness and harmony. Part of Advent's complexity is that it embraces in its celebration past, present and future: the One who came, the Presence of One who is with us and within us, and a Coming yet to be. It is about a birth and a parousia, which means both a presence beyond/within and a coming. It expresses and celebrates an essential element in christian experience and christian faith. We are an Advent people: 'we wait in joyful hope for the coming of our Saviour, Jesus Christ.'

This is not an aspect of the christian faith that the average christian is keenly aware of and the Advent season can slip by without making much impact. The first part is often dominated by pictures of a law-court general judgement and emphasis on preparing for a 'happy death'. The second part often focusses entirely on preparation for the birth of Jesus in Bethlehem, without much clarity on what this means *now,* and with heavy emphasis on morality, on 'being good' as a preparation. Looking at Advent through its symbolism and through the images presented to us in the liturgy of the season creates a somewhat different understanding from that frequently presented in Advent preaching and catechesis.

Advent liturgy of the word is full of images. Images are simply pictures in words: sometimes an evocative word or two, sometimes a vivid detailed description. Whether through economical Matisse-like sketch, impressionistic dabs of colour or careful realistic still-life or landscape; whether through delicate vignette or bold sweeping strokes, every picture says something, tells a story. Rather, every picture says many things, tells many stories. Every picture, if we let it, says something to each of us, tells each of us a different story. For this reason I do not intend to *explain* Advent images in detail but rather to make a case for listening to the images and their many possible stories, and responding personally. I would suggest that it is well worth being alert for and keenly aware of images in the scripture readings and other texts, respecting them and valuing them. If we are in a position to influence others' approach to these texts we might encourage them to do the same, rather than always giving an explanation which may in effect inhibit other people's personal response.

Imagery networks
Many powerful poems and dramas have a firm framework of images and symbols which immensely strengthens the more overt and visible structure and gives it a deeper dimension. Images catch echoes set up by previous images. Symbols and images reinforce and enrich each other. They set up resonances with each other and also with our whole store of images from our experience, our memories, our reading, our reflection on scripture, our participation in liturgy, and from the rituals of our daily life. This is why every image tells each of us a different story. The network of images and symbols is often what enables a great play to mean more than

it seems to say, to have a depth not explained by its characters and plot. This is true also of a good single Advent celebration, as of a poem; it is true of a whole Advent season celebrated with sensitivity, as of a fully developed drama.

In a poem or a play, symbols and imagery may reveal what the work is really about, what it actually says, sometimes without the conscious intention of the author. So such a network of images is well worth taking seriously. It may catch the full meaning as nothing else will. In the case of the whole liturgy of the Advent season, the network is extremely rich and varied, complex and intricate. It is not necessary, nor even desirable, to deal with it at the rational analytic level; it is desirable, specially for liturgical leaders, to be aware that the imagery network is there, that it has potential power and immense spiritual value. Even within one celebration the texts may provide a tissue of interlinked images which it would be a pity to spoil by changing a text. The responsorial psalm, for example, both on Sundays and weekdays, is almost always closely and beautifully linked to the first reading especially. Often this is quite obvious, sometimes a little more subtle. For example, Sunday 1, Year 2 has a reading from Isaiah 63-64 with Psalm 79. Phrases of the psalm take up images from the reading:

O shepherd of Israel, hear us.
(Why, Lord, leave us to stray from your way?)

O Lord rouse up your might; O Lord, come to our help.
(Oh, that you would tear the heavens open and come down.)

Let your face shine on us and we shall be saved.
(For you hid your face from us and gave us up to the
     power of our sins.)

Visit this vine and protect it.
(We have all withered like leaves.)

May your hand be on the man you have chosen.
(We the clay, you the potter.)

The network of images will proclaim something of its

message almost inevitably, but its effectiveness can be helped or hindered just as the power of the imagery in a play can be largely lost or greatly enhanced, depending on the sensitivity and understanding of the producer and how the actors interpret their lines. Apart from being weakened by poor production, the impact of the imagery of the Advent liturgy can be lost or the message scrambled by being ignored, misinterpreted or contradicted in the introduction, hymns, homily and so on. While the symbols and imagery remain fresh and full of power, some of the interpretations given have become cliché. These clichés, coming again and again as expected, can blot out the images and deaden our response. They have narrowed the meaning and scope of the scripture passages. The explanations are remembered and the images forgotten. People have been taught that they ought to listen to the homily and take it seriously; they have generally not been taught to listen to the images and take them at least equally seriously. It would be in the spirit of Advent if the as-expected, all-too-familiar and all-too-easily-recognised were to give way to the unexpected, the surprise!

Appreciation of the poetry of Advent means taking it on its own terms. This means not trying to turn an 'Ode to a Nightingale' into a treatise on ornithology! It is a pity to turn the poetry of the prophets immediately into a treatise on theology. It would be a shame to turn beautiful Advent prophetic poetry into a moral lecture. Nothing kills poetry more effectively than moralising. For that matter perhaps nothing kills the Gospel, the 'good news', more effectively than moralising! Ordinarily in our liturgy poetry tends to be overlooked or underestimated. If it is considered at all it is considered peripheral, if not totally unnecessary, or even 'soft'. Logical analytic theology and dogma are what is considered valuable as a basis for faith. But the poet can crystalise in words and images a human experience and a vision of reality. A religious poet crystalises a religious experience and a religious vision. This experience and this vision are opened to us if we open ourselves to them. To allow imagination and intuition to act in response to scriptural Advent poetry is to create the possibility of a deeper and more wholehearted understanding and commitment.

Letting the images speak
Perhaps because our priorities are set in a 'masculine' mode, there is an almost universal tendency to comment on poetic images in scriptures from a firm and fixed theological, dogmatic or moral stance. What would happen if we simply opened ourselves to the poetry and let the images 'comment on' — and even correct? — our theological theory, our understanding of salvation, our whole concept of what it is to be a christian, what christianity as a world religion is about, what celebrating Advent is about? What if we allowed Advent imagery to influence our idea of christian piety and spirituality instead of imposing dogmatic and moral interpretations on it?

On Sunday III, Year 3, we have a reading from Zephaniah 3:

> Shout with joy, daughter of Zion. Israel shout aloud!
> . . . The Lord, the king of Israel, is in your midst; you
> have no more evil to fear . . . The Lord your God is in your
> midst. He will exult with joy over you, he will renew you
> by his love; he will dance with shouts of joy for you as on
> a day of festival.

An introductory note in a guide to the liturgy of this Sunday says: 'The picture of God dancing with delight makes us smile.' It does, but only if we *see* it! The note was written by someone who saw the image and was struck by it. How often has it passed us by? If we see it and fill it in for ourselves (what kind of dance? how dressed? . . .), it may make a lasting difference. I suspect our concept of God may never be the same again!

On the other hand, a suggested introduction to a reading from Isaiah II (Sunday II, Year I) says: 'Isaiah promises a great leader, the Messiah, who will bring perfect justice and peace. Jesus is that leader.' The reading, Isaiah 11:1-10, paints a wonderful series of pictures of perfect justice, idyllic harmony and peace. If we are alert and listen to that introduction and then listen to the poetic images of a new Eden, we must surely ask the question, 'So Jesus has come — but where is this justice, peace and harmony? We are far indeed from paradise, and we are puzzled.' In dealing with the prophetic first reading of the Advent Masses, we may hear it baldly stated that the reading refers to the coming of the Messiah in the birth of Jesus, as if the rest were obvious, could be taken for granted and followed automatically. Everything has been accomplished; present reality seems to be ignored. What are these readings actually saying? Have they any significance for us now and what we are supposed to be doing? Are they about some distant past or some distant future? Has something more to happen before this perfect peace reigns? Is there another coming of the Messiah? What does that mean? Have we any role to play? It is certainly difficult to give a simple introduction that is not too simplistic. One helpful possibility might be to take all the readings of one year's Advent celebration, or at least all the Sunday readings and work on them *together* as a unit. Then Mass introductions, introductions to readings, homilies could all be prepared in such a way that they meshed with each other, so that a coherent if complex notion of what Advent is about might be built up gradually, with the help of, rather than in spite of, the scriptural imagery.

Another fairly typical example. In a recent homily guide I find as introduction to the Gospel: 'The gospel urges us to prepare for the coming of Christ. We know not the day or the hour when the Lord will call us to himself.' So, 'the coming of Christ' is our death? The gospel passage this introduces is Luke 21:25-28, 34-36 (Sunday I, Year 3), which speaks of 'signs in the sun and the moon and the stars', 'nations in agony bewildered by the clamour of the ocean and its waves', the 'powers of heaven' being shaken and 'the Son of Man coming in a cloud with power and great glory.' It is worth visualising and feeling this powerful apocalptic imagery but I scarcely need to do that to know that it does not refer to my death! Even allowing for the exaggeration of the genre this must surely be about something of far greater moment to the world, to the christian people, and even to me personally as a christian, than the passing in death of any individual, even myself. The gospel verses chosen go on:

> Watch yourselves, or your hearts will be coarsened by debauchery and drunkenness and the cares of life, and that day will be sprung on you suddenly like a trap.

This gives scope for moral exhortation, and it does refer to individuals, but what is 'that day'? It may be relevant to the day of a person's death but in the context is that what it means? Listening to the image would at least raise the question.

Relevant to several readings in the first two weeks of Advent, and to many homilies thereon, is the question 'Did Jesus in the gospels ever talk about the death of individuals as "the coming of the Lord" or the day when he would come again or "the day of the Lord"?' When he talks about the householder being ready for the unexpected thief, or the servants left in charge who must be ready when the master returns, is he merely telling us to be ready for the day of our death? Is this what the context, the imagery and the overall teaching of Jesus indicates? If not, perhaps we should think more of what Jesus is talking about in these passages, now almost invariably referred to the need to be ready for our death. II Peter 3 (Sunday II, Year 2) startlingly combines the 'thief' image with the apocalyptic:

> The day of the Lord will come like a thief, and then with a roar the sky will vanish, the elements will catch fire and fall apart, the earth and all that it contains will be burnt up.

Some thief! This does suggest again that the 'thief' is the unexpected and not simply death.

This imagery and the whole imagery of Advent leads overwhelmingly to the conclusion that as christians we have something very much more important to think about and to work for, something of far greater moment to be concerned about in looking to the future, than merely preparing for death and taking care not to be caught on the wrong foot. The Second Coming I am called to long for and work for is bigger than me; I am not the central figure. We are called to a far greater and more constructive enterprise than polishing our haloes, as it were, so that we will pass muster at some great passing out parade! The point of the 'thief' and the 'householder' imagery is the unexpectedness, the unlooked-for. His coming had, has in our day to day lives, and apparently will have in the end, an element of surprise, of the unlooked-for. When he came in Bethlehem many who thought they were waiting and ready missed him because he came in the 'wrong' place, in the 'wrong' way, in the 'wrong' circles. As we try to live our lives in faith and hope there is always the possibility that we shall keep on missing him because he keeps on coming in the wrong way, at the wrong time, in the wrong places, among the wrong people, by-passing our narrow preconceived ideas. That is one reason why being open to the fullness of Advent imagery and symbol may be important; it, too, may by-pass our pre-conceived ideas if we let it.

Visual interpretation

While there is some danger in trying to make visible the poetic images of the biblical writers, pictures may help. Hearing the images in words and letting the people create and re-create them in their own imaginations may be best. The child who preferred radio to television because the pictures were better had a valid and relevant point. Nevertheless some of the imagery and its meaning in its context may be so far outside people's personal experience that we need help for our imaginations. One good way to provide this is to show a series of slides. This is not easy or even possible in most churches but it can be done in other settings: at scripture services, prayer meetings, retreats, in the classroom, at liturgy preparation meetings and so on. Whatever the setting, the slides or other visual aids and any accompanying sound should be aesthetically and technically good, and any apparatus used should be at least adequate. Slides can accompany a reading or be a meditation before or after it with music. They can be used between two readings of the same passage. This provides a good combination: letting the reading itself speak, then feeding the imagination, and finally letting the reading speak again. This provides help by building up a wider repertoire for the imagination to call on now and in the future and enriches our understanding while leaving everyone free to deal with the reading itself by themselves.

Clearly this imaging for others has to be done sensitively and by someone who has a good background knowledge. It calls for an understanding of the passage, personal reflection on it and the artistic ability to express this understanding and reflection in a series of images. This is an interpretation of the passage as much as a verbal interpretation would be, but interpretation through further images is far less limited and limiting; it is more open-ended and evokes a more personal response. It can bring out the relevance of the passage through using contemporary images. Let us not fall into the 'romantic' trap that only 'lovely' images are poetic or spiritual. By all means when interpreting biblical poetry, whether in visual images or in words, let us see contemporary scenes including urban, industrial, Third World — and including the unlovely, the shocking, the painful and the violent, when appropriate, as well as the beautiful. In providing a series of visual images a large part of what we are doing is translating the biblical images into our culture and our language. The *words* have been translated for us but that is only a beginning. Images should be translated when necessary with the same care that we give to translating the words.

Extra-biblical images
We think of Advent as pre-eminently the season of messianic prophesy, and we think especially of Isaiah. Prophesy and poetry are very closely akin. It is by no means accidental

that many of the biblical prophets are poets. The link between prophesy and poetry did not end with the canonical scriptures. In the breviary appendix of poems for optional use in the Prayer of the Church, there is little or no Advent poetry — one possible-Advent poem. This is surprising because Advent themes abound in poetry, including modern and contemporary poetry. Today's 'New Age' thinking, expressed in poetry and elsewhere, is basically Advent thinking, but the language may not be Advent cliché. As an aside here, it is sad that so many people to whom 'New Age' thinking appeals become alienated and leave their churches because they believe their thinking is unorthodox and has no place there. Genuine Advent preaching and teaching would in many cases appeal to them, hold them and enthuse them.

One way to enrich our symbols, myths, rituals, traditional biblical images, is to listen to later poets reflect on and refresh them. When these poets speak out of our own culture or our own time, or both, they can in a very real sense bring the images 'home' to us. I think for instance of lines by Tim Jackson, a contemporary Irish poet, from his poem 'Parousia':

Yet there is hope for a new synthesis
Drawing together the strands of creation,
Converging together under the banner of Christ.
It is happening, quietly, inevitably,
Trickling into all corners like the rising tide.
Many are too heavy to lift into the new dimension,
Drowned in the density of their many necessities,
Trapped in the tensions of life's trivia.
Yet some even now hear the whisper and slap of running
    water
And work and work, knowing that soon
Their life will lift from the inertia of history
And they will sail, singing, with the storm of his coming.

Rich as our scriptural writings are, we do not have to confine ourselves to biblical images. If we really celebrate Advent, *live* Advent, we will come across or come up with others of our own. Some may be private, some public; some purely personal, some to be shared. Sharing our images is a wonderful and profound way of faith-sharing and there is no better way of building a faith community. One contemporary 'public' Advent symbol which is very beautiful and very powerful is that first vision of the earth as seen from space, an exquisite blue-green spherical gem set in vast blue-black space. The sight very deeply moved those who saw it and they shared their vision with us, and its meaning for them. Not only for them but for thousands of those who merely saw the television pictures or photographs and heard the astronaut's words, it at once became a powerful symbol of the unity of humankind, and the focus of hope for future global peace and harmony. It is a fitting extension for our day of the Old Testament messianic images. It has motivated many, as our messianic images have not always motivated christians, to dedicate themselves to making that peace and unity a reality. It is certainly one of the great contemporary Advent symbols and need not be left outside church circles.

For some, I know, the United Nations building in New York is an Advent symbol of hope for 'messianic' peace and unity in the world. It is a symbol sadly flawed by failure but one of my own Advent symbols is at the heart of that building. In the centre of the small silent circular meditation room, designed in its present form by Dag Hammarksjold, is a great rough-hewn sphere of rock. There one is not alone. As II Peter tells us, 'with the Lord a day is as a thousand years, and a thousand years as a day', so all who had ever come there to pause, to pray or even simply to long for the peace of the world were there together. It is a 'Jerusalem' symbol. They came, maybe not in the streams the prophet saw but at least in trickles, from all corners of the earth, of all creeds and cultures and colours. And they have brought a 'glory' to that spot and there, in some small measure and in pledge, 'the Lord draws all nations together for the peace of God's kingdom'.

Another image that has stayed with me and with at least

a few other people, and has got itself enmeshed in the Advent network, is a contemporary image of a very ancient symbol coming from our neolithic past: a splendid photograph taken a year or two ago at Newgrange. It shows the sun at the moment of sunrise on the winter solstice shining straight through a small aperture in the massive stone walls and between great standing slabs of rock, to light up the passage-way and flood the whole inner cavern with golden light. It stirs something in the soul and speaks of the triumph of light, of hope and exultation, and joins us, back through thousands of years, to generations who were keenly aware of the dark-ness and celebrated the light. So to celebrate the sun when at its lowest and weakest, when most peoples saw it as dying, seems a wonderful expression of hope. It is a resurrection image, but then resurrection imagery is always so closely intertwined with Advent imagery that the two are inseparable, and that is as it should be. It is always the Risen Christ that we are celebrating.

Beyond and within ourselves

The complexity of Advent means that its images can be applied at different levels. In much Advent thinking they are referred almost exclusively to the historical past (the birth of Jesus) and to the personal future (our death). The scale of the imagery with its vast sweep of plains and valleys and mountains, deserts and oceans, multitudes and peoples, cosmic chaos and cosmic harmony, calls us beyond the historic past to the whole sweep of time – past, present and future. It calls us beyond the individual to the universal, to the whole universe and all its people. It calls us beyond ourselves to the community of believers. All the scripture readings are addressed to a *people* or a *community of believers* and not directly to any individual as such. Getting us to widen the scope of our hope beyond ourselves may be part of the coming of the Reign of God, as Coleridge saw:

No common centre Man, no common sire
Knoweth. A sordid solitary thing

Mid countless brethren, with a lonely heart
Through courts and cities the smooth savage roams
Feeling himself, his own low self, the whole
When he by sacred sympathy might make
The Whole one Self. Self that no alien knows . . .
Self, spreading still. Oblivious of its own
Yet all of all possessing. This is faith!
This the Messiah's destined victory!

(from: 'Religious Musings')

Advent calls us beyond any narrow, individualistic, self-centred concept of salvation. Perhaps this is part of what we need to be freed from in order to be freed for selfless striving for the coming of the Kingdom.

O Key of David, who open the gates of the eternal kingdom, come to liberate from prison the captive who lives in darkness.

Albert Einstein, who had profound things to say about humanity, religion and mysticism as well as physics, saw each human being as limited in time and space but part of a great unlimited whole.

It is a delusion to think that we are separated from everyone and everything else. This delusion is a kind of prison to us, restricting us to our personal concerns and to affections of a few people nearest to us. Our task must be to free ourselves from this prison by widening our circle of compassion to embrace all living creatures and the whole of nature in its beauty.

In so far as we apply the Advent images to ourselves, they call us beyond moralism to a deep and wide spirituality, to a reaching out to full humanness and wholeness. We can apply the images inwardly to our whole being. The rapid spread and popularisation of various psychological techniques and of 'new' spiritualities means that an increasing number of people are at least becoming aware of, or have had some experience of, human growth movements, psychotherapies which use imagination, or spiritual practices which use guided imagery in meditation or prayer. These people and all those on these wavelengths or ready to tune in will almost inevitably find that the scriptural images set up conscious resonances with their own personal myths and symbols, or they find, often with delighted surprise, 'their' symbols in the biblical readings. The meanings of both are enriched and the person takes an important step towards harmony, integration and wholeness. This inner universe is a valid area in which to apply all the Advent imagery, though we should not stop there. The kingdom of God is within us but there, as in the wider universe, it has to grow and spread. In that process we may experience the apocalyptic chaos and disruption and the Messianic peace and harmony — and everything in between. Our lion may have to learn to lie down with our lamb. The medieval verse recognised this inner world and the transformation Christ's coming may bring:

You shall know him when he comes
Not by any din of drums,
Not by anything he wears,
Nor by the vantage of his airs;
  Not by his gown,
  Nor by his crown,
But his coming known shall be
By the holy harmony
That his presence makes in thee.

The Advent Wreath and symbolic actions

The Advent wreath is perhaps the only material Advent symbol found in most churches. For most of us it is a comparatively recent addition to our Advent celebration. The material element of a symbol tends to be basically simple. The original delicate symbolic value can easily be spoilt or smothered by extraneous or irrelevant accretions. This has already sometimes happened to the Advent wreath where the symbolism was not appreciated or respected. The wreath is a circle of evergreens bearing four candles. The *circle* represents the cycle of time, and is a symbol of perfection, of eternity and of fidelity. The essential point about the wreath is that it is a ring of *evergreens,* symbol of faithfulness and of hope in the cold, bare days of winter. The four candles represent the four weeks, but also all the time till the coming of Christ. The progressively growing light (one candle the first week, two the second, and so on) expresses heightening hope and expectation, and the building up of light till the coming of *the* Light. It represents the gradual coming of the Kingdom building up to the final triumph of the coming of the Reign of God. As we light the candles we are expressing our hope in this and our commitment to work to bring it about.

The quality of the material symbol is always important if it is to express the symbolic meaning. The wreath and candles need to be sufficiently large to make an impact in the space concerned. A small wreath in a large church will be insignificant. It is *essentially* a wreath of *evergreens,* not of flowers or berries, and not (perish the thought!) of plastic imitations. Even if the greenery is arranged in a moisture-retaining medium, the wreath will need to be watered and sprayed to keep it fresh and clean. It will need to be renewed if it is to remain fresh and green throughout Advent. A wreath of faded, dusty, dried-up or dead greenery can scarcely be a symbol of hope! The four candles should be the same size and shape and colour. There is nothing sacrosanct about purple, and the idea of three purple and one rose or pink is an example of an arbitrary and irrelevant complication coming from rules about Advent Mass vestments and is merely a distraction. Finally, the *lighting* of the candles is part of the symbolism and should be done visibly and in a dignified way as a minor ritual which is given appropriate time and space. It is best done by a comprehending and sensitive adult or group of adults, or by a family, rather than perfunctorily by an obedient but uncomprehending altar boy. The lighting can be done in silence letting the gesture speak for itself, or accompanied by music or a suitable song or chant.

Most often the Advent wreath just disappears at Christmas. More and more, however, it is carried on with symbolic logic into the Christmas celebration. On Christmas Eve before midnight Mass a large white candle, perhaps flower-adorned, is placed ceremoniously in the centre of the wreath with its lighted candles, to symbolise the long-awaited Light of Christ come into our world. A suitable further extension is for the wreath to remain for the whole Christmastide celebration with all its candles lighted and its evergreens now intertwined with flowers or surmounted by a wreath of flowers and berries to symbolise our joy, and hope fulfilled.

This can be linked to another symbolic action which I have seen several times in connection with or in place of the usual procession to place the infant in the crib. This action is the lighting of a large Christmas candle — a smaller or slender version of the Paschal candle — to the chant of the Easter 'Lumen Christi' or other similar praise of the Light of Christ. The candle is then carried to the crib and/or to a prominent stand in the sanctuary, with or without the Advent wreath on it. Ideally there will be pauses or 'stations' for candles of all the ministers and of all the people to be lighted, after the manner of the Easter Vigil on which the ceremony is based. The celebration of the coming of the Light might express the meaning of Advent and Christmas better than simply laying the child in the manger, and lessen the limiting emphasis on the birth in Bethlehem and the consequent Baby Jesus cult. The obvious overtones and resonances with Easter bring home non-verbally that it is the Risen Lord we celebrate even at Christmas. Our taking up the light with our little candles suggests our mission, individually and collectively, to be the light of the world, to contribute to the growth and spread of the light until it drives out all darkness and the unconquerable Sun shines unobstructed in us and through us in the whole world. These symbolic actions take in all levels of the Coming — past, present and future.

Some threads of the network
The best-known Advent image is 'preparing the way'. The

prophetic picture was of a great, level, raised road cutting across the undulating desert hills; a royal road, an easy way, a ready way. Our literal modern equivalent would be road improvement work which cuts out sharp bends, unexpected bumps and dangerous bridges, thus making things easier and speedier for the traveller. What does the image mean? How do we speed the coming of the Lord? This image gains prominence by being taken up by John the Baptist in the New Testament, but it occurs comparatively few times in the Advent season. One of those times, with typical Advent ambivalence, it is 'reversed' and it is the Lord who prepares the way for his people!

> For God has decreed the flattening
> of each high mountain of the everlasting hills,
> the filling of the valleys to make the ground level
> so that Israel can walk in safety under the glory of God.
> And the forests and every fragrant tree will provide shade
> for Israel at the command of God.
>
> (Baruch 5:6-8, Sunday II, Year 3)

What does this say? And does it colour the reverse use of the image?

This lovely passage has a faint echo of Eden before the Fall. This particular thread runs through a great many of the images. It is difficult, and fortunately neither necessary nor specially useful, to disentangle the threads that go to make up the image network. It is easier to notice some characteristics of the images. One of these is the use of startling contrast, between power and gentleness, for instance. Thundering storms become gentle dew; triumphant warrior becomes, without transition, a compassionate shepherd:

> Here is the Lord coming with power,
> his arm subduing all things to him.
> The prize of his victory is with him,
> his trophies all go before him.
> He is like a shepherd feeding his flock,
> gathering lambs in his arms,

149

holding them against his breast
and leading to their rest the mother ewes.

(Isaiah 40:9-11. Sunday II, Year 2)

Putting these two together almost defeats our imagination, but it is worth trying. We may remember this when we come to pray:

> O Wisdom of the Most High, ordering all things with strength and gentleness, come and teach us the way of truth.

Another characteristic is a certain exaggeration, exuberance. The desert does not just flower, as deserts do in spring; it becomes luxuriant and produces cedars like Lebanon. The lame will not just walk, they will leap and dance. Running through many and varied images and their exuberance is a clear suggestion, surfacing again and again, of a new and more wonderful Creation, another and more perfect Paradise. Echoes of Genesis resound. Edwin Muir, in his poem 'Transfiguration', takes up a theme beloved of the Fathers of the Church and of medieval hymn-writers when he runs the film backwards to a New Eden:

> But he will come again, it's said, though not
> Unwanted and unsummoned; for all things,
> Beasts of the field and woods and rocks and seas
> And all mankind from end to end of the earth
> Will call him in one voice. In our own time,
> Some way, or at a time when time is ripe,
> Then he will come, Christ the uncrucified,
> Christ the discrucified, his death undone,
> His agony unmade, his cross dismantled,
> Glad to be so — and the tormented wood
> Will cure its hurt and grow into a tree
> In a green springing corner of young Eden.

The image that occurs most often by far is that of Jerusalem and Mount Zion. Like all genuine symbols it is rooted in concrete reality. Jerusalem was a city not altogether unlike other cities; other cities too in the ancient world had their temples. Mount Zion itself is an insignificant little hillock. When Jerusalem and Zion became symbols they were invested with meaning and they grew in grandeur in the people's imagination, especially during the Exile. The physical site provided a place for the symbol to strike root, a space in which it could grow. Mount Zion as brought into the vision of God's plan, as focus of the people's hopes, became a magnificent mountain, another and mightier Horeb, as we are reminded by constant allusions to that other mountain of the Lord. Zion towers above all mountains, drawing all peoples by its magnetic power and its mystery. Peoples came streaming from all directions to hear the Law, to learn the Way of the Lord, and that Way is peace. Jerusalem is *the* city on a hill which cannot be hidden, which radiates light to all the world, drawing all to it. As with much Advent imagery, there is an ambivalence, a kind of two-way movement: the glory of Jerusalem draws the peoples to her; the coming of the peoples *is* the glory of the city.

Unless we choose more or less to ignore a notable portion of the Advent readings, we have to give meaning to these Jerusalem-Zion images. They are still very powerful symbols for Jews; what about christians? An Irish playwright reminds us: 'It is not the past that shapes us but images of the past embodied in language'. (Brian Friel, *Translations*). The Jewish people have been formed and shaped by these and other images; to a greater extent than we are aware, so have we. Where and what is our 'Jerusalem'? The over-simple answer often given in introductions to 'Jerusalem' readings is: 'Jerusalem is the Church.' In what sense? To very many people in the pews 'the Church' is an institution and a hierarchy; with that in mind, the readings do not 'fit', do not make much sense. Is all this Zion poetry more or less empty rhetoric? Is 'Jerusalem' just a castle in the air? Has all this somehow 'happened'? Has it become a reality? Is it becoming a reality? Or is it going to become a reality some day? If so, when? where? how? It may be helpful to encourage more people to ask these questions for themselves and of themselves and to grope about seeking answers in their own faith, theology, spirituality and psyche, rather than offer them very limited answers from outside.

Jerusalem is a nexus linking many other images. It is a central knot in the network of imagery. Many other images are referred to Jerusalem or Zion, connected with Jerusalem or closely parallel the Jerusalem theme. The image of the Shoot from the stock of Jesse, for example, parallels the Zion images, as well as being part of winter-spring and kingship images. 'The branch of the Lord shall be beauty and glory'. Like Jerusalem, it

shall stand as a signal to the peoples.
It will be sought out by the nations
and its home will be glorious.

(Isaiah 11:10. Tuesday, Week I)

'Clothing' imagery usually refers to Jerusalem. Integrity is often a cloak; lack of it is 'filthy clothing'. Jerusalem is to 'put off her dress of sorrow and distress' — like Synge's Deirdre who has 'put away sorrow like a shoe that is worn out and muddy.' She is to 'put on the beauty of the glory of God for ever.' That could be Synge, too, but it is Baruch 5:1.

Paul also has a 'clothing' image though a very different one. He rouses us at the start of the season with a 'get up and go' routine. (Rom 13, Sunday I, Year I.) Night is almost over, day is at hand. We are to wake up, take off the things of darkness, put on our 'armour' and appear, be seen, in the light. We are, in fact, to 'put on the Lord Jesus Christ' — and presumably go out into our day to day world dressed in Christ, appearing as Christ, to *be* Christ by having his mind and acting like him. Maybe this striking image sums up much of the meaning of Advent: the present coming and ourselves as link between the first and second comings.

In Advent a vision is presented to us. As we celebrate the season year after year a complex and many faceted vision is gradually built up as we become aware of, look at, reflect upon, absorb and recreate inwardly for ourselves a whole mosaic of images. It is a vision of awe-inspiring proportions, full of joy and hope, of unfathomable perfection and wonder. All the symbols and images together add up to an attempt to imagine what is unimaginable because it is beyond our widest experience and our wildest expectation. But to believe in it, to hope in it, to work for it, to be part of it, is of the essence of what it is to be a christian.